Saint-Laurent

Montréal's Main

PIERRE ANCTIL

Saint-Laurent

Montréal's Main

Montréal Museum of
Archaeology and History

Baraka
Books

SEPTENTRION

This publication is based on research carried out for the exhibition of the same name, mounted by Pointe-à-Callière, the Montréal Museum of Archaeology and History, and presented there from April 17 to October 27, 2002.
Director of Exhibitions, Marie Émond; Project Manager, Sylvie Durand; Scientific validation, Paul-André Linteau; Publication advisors, Plurimedia Communications; Iconographic research, Christine Conciatori, Nathalie Simard, Pierre Wilson; English translation and proof-reading, Terry Knowles and Pamela Ireland

ACKNOWLEDGEMENTS
Pointe-à-Callière, the Montréal Museum of Archaeology and History, wishes to thank the Ministère des Relations avec les citoyens et de l'Immigration for its valuable assistance, as well as the following institutions, companies, associations and individuals:

André Brassard
Archives nationales de France
Archives nationales du Québec
Archives of the Canadian Jewish Congress
Archives of the Canadian Pacific Railway
Archives of the International
    Ladies' Garment Workers' Union
Archives of the Société de transport de Montréal
Bibliothèque nationale du Québec
Canadian Broadcasting Corporation
Canadian Centre for Architecture
Catherine Fung Collection
Cinémathèque québécoise
City of Montréal
Concordia University Archives

Danielle Bérard, photographer
Direction des Archives de France
Edward Hillel, photographer
Robert Hébert, photographer @ Sodart
La Presse
Margie Gillis Dance Foundation,
    Annie Leibovitz, photographer
McClelland & Steweart Ltd.
McCord Museum of Canadian History
McGill University
Michel Régner, photographer
Ministère de la Défense, Service historique
    de l'Armée de terre, France
Molson family

Musée de la civilisation
Musée de la Gaspésie
National Archives of Canada
National Gallery of Canada
Nicole Léger, photographer
Rubenstein Bros. Co. Inc.
Sam Tata, photographer
Sony Music Entertainment
Southam Inc./*The Gazette*
Stella Collection
Théâtre de la manufacture, La Licorne
Yivo Institute, New York

Cover page photo: Packed with passengers, a row of trams sets off from the corner of Sainte-Catherine Street to conquer the Main. Behind them, on the west side of the street, can be seen the imposing profile of the Monument national. Archives of the Société de transport de Montréal, 1-917-006.
Back cover photo: In a swirling gust of snow, passengers hurry to board a bus on the corner of des Pins Avenue. The image recalls the Main's longstanding role as a crossroads of cultures and a passage through the heart of the city. Photograph: Danielle Bérard, 1986.

Baraka Books and Les éditions du Septentrion wish to thank the Canada Council for the Arts and the Société de développement des entreprises culturelles du Québec (SODEC) for support of their publishing programs, as well as the Government of Quebec for its tax credit program for book publishing. We are also grateful for financial support received from the Government of Canada through the Book Publishing Industry Development Program (BPIDP).

Legal deposit – 4th quarter 2009
Bibliothèque et Archives nationales du Québec
Library and Archives Canada
ISBN 978-0-9812405-8-9

The "Main" is an exceptional street, and has been ever since it originated as Chemin Saint-Laurent, a winding pathway through the woods and fertile fields of the island of Montréal. Even in those days it was a public thoroughfare, belonging to everyone. Over time it has remained a place of transit, untamed and elusive, like an arm of the St. Lawrence River itself, flowing northward into the heart of the island. It is no coincidence that the port of Montréal developed at the foot of the "Main" and no surprise that waves of immigrants have regularly swept up it since the late 19th century...

Translated excerpt from André-G. Bourassa and Jean-Marc Larrue, *Les Nuits de la Main.* Montréal: VLB éditeur, 1993, p. 183.

Table of Contents

Boulevard of Dreams

"Exceptional!" we would say of someone who has managed to transcend the ordinary and achieve the extraordinary, to surpass the individual and accomplish the universal. In many ways, Saint-Laurent Boulevard deserves a similar tribute. Few if any other arteries in Canada can boast such a concentration of history and humanity. Montréal's Main seems to have seen and heard it all, to know all of the city's past—and even its future, since it is here that the commercial, social, cultural, artistic and even technological trends that are part of our everyday lives have so often emerged.

Yes, Saint-Laurent is an exceptionally rich subject. Yet it doesn't flaunt its wealth. For while money and ambition are often front and centre in the hip bars and restaurants on the Main, its strength lies much more in its mysterious ability to serve as the melting pot of human cultures, dreams and hopes. The Main is part of everyone, it belongs to everyone, in its own way it is everyone.

We must express our gratitude to Pierre Anctil, a recognized expert in the humanities who has a special interest in Montréal urban studies and a great knowledge and appreciation of our cultural communities. He has succeeded here in throwing new light on the events, figures and movements that have transformed a little country road into the diverse and captivating Main we know today. He leads us through the years as Chemin Saint-Laurent, the walled town's sole pressure valve toward the north of the Island, gradually became lined with homes, welcomed stores and factories and was renamed Main Street and then Boulevard, and as its namesake suburb overflowed into new villages. We watch wave upon wave of immigrants from every continent arriving in the harbour and drifting northward. No passive flow, though—anything but! This was an active current, shaping the "banks" of this other St. Lawrence river, as each culture left its imprint in the form of new languages, new flavours and new resilience. We see how the arts and pleasures that make the modern-day Main a showcase of creation and entertainment in Montréal have long been concentrated here, including its illicit attractions, as if to better protect the tranquillity of the rest of the city. We come to understand that the Main knows all about business, from the most respectable to the most dubious, and that its shady reputation goes back a long way...

Over the years, different city administrations have tried to beat the Main into submission, to sanitize it, to purge it of its vices and illicit traffic of all kinds. Others have razed entire blocks in an effort to make it conform, to create something more "normal"—more beautiful, in a word. But the Main possesses another kind of beauty. And where some people see orderliness as tangible evidence of prosperity, this urban jungle—hot, throbbing and never sleeping—replies: I'm here. I'm here to stay. I bring fashions into being even before anyone knows they are fashions. I give shelter to creative spirits who can see the soul in my abandoned factories. I propose and I dispose. I draw sustenance from the anonymous and creative masses that keep choosing me as home. My architectural heritage is admittedly rather eclectic. But most of all, my heritage consists of dreams, modest beginnings, brilliant ideas and fertile disorder.

In 1998, as the author reminds us, the Historic Sites and Monuments Board of Canada declared the Main a historic district of national significance, from the River up to Jean-Talon Street. On behalf of Pointe-à-Callière, the Montréal Museum of Archaeology and History, whose foremost goal is to help people better know and appreciate our city, I am delighted that this rigorously documented book will give us a clearer view of this very old and constantly new artery.

With its clear narrative, striking anecdotes and impressively thorough analysis, this book will introduce you to a Saint-Laurent Boulevard that opens its arms to everyone and yet never quite reveals all its secrets. Through its abundant and well-explained illustrations, you will witness the countless metamorphoses of this street that defies categorization. Some have left traces, but most have been swept away by the powerful wind of change that is constantly blowing along the Main—perhaps its only truly permanent feature. Then, with the new-found vision imparted by Pierre Anctil, go back and stroll along Montréal's boulevard of dreams. You're sure to appreciate it even more.

FRANCINE LELIÈVRE
Executive Director
Pointe-à-Callière
Montréal Museum of Archaeology and History

A Vehicle for Modernity

Montréal's geography played a large part in the birth and development of the long urban artery that would become Saint-Laurent Boulevard in the 20th century. The St. Lawrence River, surrounding Montréal on all sides, for many years funnelled all travel into the backcountry of North America along one majestic route. Land communications on the island would likewise largely be directed along a single route in the early decades of the French regime. Like the River, which channelled all the colony's military and trading activities as it penetrated westward, settlement as it pushed toward the northern part of the island and beyond would

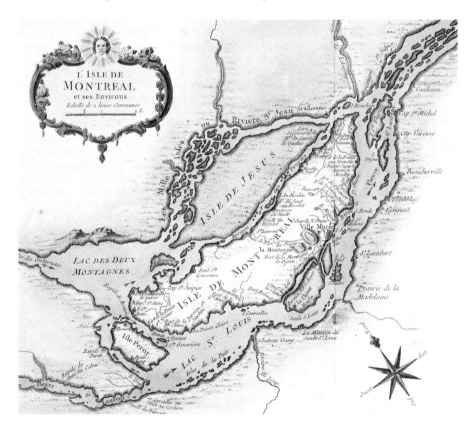

MAP OF THE ISLAND OF MONTRÉAL AND ENVIRONS (DETAIL), AFTER JACQUES-NICOLAS BELLIN, 1764
Surrounded as it is by a number of waterways, the Montréal archipelago is strategically located in North America. It funnelled all travel into the interior of the continent. Because ships were blocked from going any farther by the Lachine Rapids, in 1642 explorers, colonists, soldiers and merchants founded an outpost here that would grow into the town of Montréal.

be concentrated along one road for many years, giving it a monopoly over all significant travel on the island. Chemin de Saint-Laurent, running at right angles to the shoreline and bearing the same name as the River, played the same founding role and had the same symbolic significance for the town as the great waterway did for the entire continent.

A Vital Thoroughfare

The predominance of Chemin de Saint-Laurent would later be challenged by other major north-south arteries, like Côte-des-Neiges and Papineau, but none would manage to dislodge it from its place in Montrealers' collective imagination. The Anglophones who dominated the city in the 19th century in fact dubbed it the "Main," and the name stuck: it was adopted by every one of the immigrant communities that Montréal welcomed in subsequent decades.

After all, this artery had always been a thoroughfare around which the town and later the city itself grew up. Later, it would also attract immigrant communities from the Old World, who settled and flourished there. By crossing what were virgin spaces in the eyes of the European colonizers and carrying new populations and new visions and ideas northward from the harbour into the hinterland, the Main acted as a vehicle for modernity. Like the river flowing at its feet, this road opened up new vistas in the urban landscape and helped shape the Montréal we know today.

Birth of a Great Urban Artery

IN THE BEGINNING, IN THE EARLY 18TH CENTURY, THE MAIN WAS NO MORE THAN A COUNTRY ROAD RUNNING NORTH-SOUTH THROUGH THE FARMING HINTERLAND SPREAD OUT AROUND THE ISLAND. IT OWES ITS HISTORICAL IMPORTANCE TO THE FRENCH AUTHORITIES' FEARS OF INVASION AND THEIR DECISION TO LIMIT THE NUMBER OF GATES IN THE TOWN WALLS.

MONTRÉAL, THE STRATEGIC GATEWAY OF NEW FRANCE

Although Montréal was founded in 1642 by a religious society that sprang from the Counter-Reformation in France, within just a few years the settlement came to play a pivotal role in the fur trade between the Great Lakes region and the mother country. Utopian plans of converting Natives and the more realistic goal of using the land for farming soon gave way, after Maisonneuve's departure, to strategic imperatives: controlling the waterways leading to the interior of the continent and supplying the colony's outposts. As a result of this major shift, by the end of the 17th century Montréal had become a transportation hub for trade goods and the operational base for all French military expeditions to defend lands west of the colony. Similarly, Natives wishing to deal in any way with the French in North America also converged on Montréal.

The town served as a vital warehouse, garrison and administrative centre on the westward route, and its urban development soon reflected these functions. Montréal's role as the logistical centre for all of New France, owing to its location at the confluence of a great many waterways, required a defensive perimeter around the town in keeping with the military imperatives of the day. The town was faced with two persistent threats in the late 17th century — attacks by Iroquois bands from the west (until the Great Peace was signed in 1701), and a European-style military invasion from the English colonies to the south. In both cases, the enemy could throw considerable numbers of men at the gates of the city, although land communication routes were too primitive to bring high-calibre artillery to bear.

To respond to this threat, French authorities erected a simple cedar palisade in 1687, and then began work on stone fortifications in 1717. Under the direction of military engineer Chaussegros de Léry, the new wall was completed in 1744, nearly thirty years later. It stood about ten metres high and consisted of a series of bastions and curtain walls, covering a 3,500-metre

**PLAN OF THE WALL AROUND THE TOWN OF MONTRÉAL AND
THE OUTLINE OF ITS FORTIFICATIONS, LOUIS FRANQUET, 1752**

Fearing an attack from the heights overlooking the town, military engineers began building a stone wall around the town in 1717. They placed only one gate on the north flank of the fortifications. From this gate, known as the *Grande Porte Saint-Laurent*, led the *Grand chemin du Roy*, soon renamed Chemin de Saint-Laurent. Its route, clearly visible on this plan, is the same as that of modern-day Montréal's Main, or Saint-Laurent Boulevard.

perimeter and incorporating the latest French architectural urban defence theories of the day. The construction of such complex defensive works had an impact not only on the French budget and Montréal taxes, but also on the development of the town itself and land use. For military reasons, there had to be a clear space of several hundred metres outside the walls to make it possible to spot and fire on approaching enemies. Such military requirements guided the spatial development of the town for several decades, and prevented other communication routes from extending outward from the walls.

The defensive works designed by Chaussegros de Léry were intended to respond to overland threats, coming from the heights on the north side of the town. Five of the eight major gates in Montréal's fortifications faced the St. Lawrence, which was itself considered a formidable obstacle to potential attackers. Because the other three defensive flanks were so vulnerable to a massed attack by land, each had just one gate. The only gate leading to the north, known as the *Grande Porte Saint-Laurent*, was finally opened in 1732. The sole route leading to the north of the Island and future farming settlements on the Saint-Laurent, Sainte-Catherine, de Liesse and des Vertus *côtes* had actually extended from the town at this point since 1717. The future Saint-Laurent Boulevard would follow the exact same route as this dirt track through the farmland north of the town.

DOLLIER DE CASSON LAYS OUT RUE SAINT-LAMBERT

The northward axis, swerving strongly to the west, taken by the *"grand chemin de Roy,"* soon to be known as Chemin de Saint-Laurent, was actually present in embryonic form more than half a century earlier. Its traces can be seen very clearly in 1672, in the urban layout traced by the owners and seigneurs of Montréal Island, appearing on a plan drawn by Dollier de Casson. Early on, the Sulpicians took an interest in imposing order on the space within the walls and deciding how it would be laid out. If the street grid of the town was not to become totally chaotic, what was needed was a strict plan from the very beginning. Indeed, the urban plan of the town that would take shape within the walls dates back to that time. In 1672, a little street named Saint-Lambert ran at right angles to Rue Notre-Dame. This minor urban street would provide the precise route for Chemin de Saint-Laurent, and later the Main, whose dazzling future would mark Montréal history in so many ways.

On all the plans of the town prepared under the French regime starting in the late 17th century, in particular the one by Chaussegros de Léry dating from 1725, the Chemin de Saint-Laurent can easily be seen running through the wall and northward. In fact, while this road was rather unprepossessing at the time, it long remained the only connection with the parishes developing on the north of the island, including the village of Saint-Laurent and beyond. Accordingly, for decades the future Saint-Laurent Boulevard served more as a means of communication across "deserts" than as an inhabited street. Indeed, it is worth noting that it was not a concession road or a route lined with farming families, but rather a link between the "*côtes*" (concessions), some of which, like Côte-des-Neiges and Côte-Sainte-Catherine, are located far from the banks of the St. Lawrence.

Farmers on Île Jésus and in the northern parts of Montréal Island simply took Chemin de Saint-Laurent to reach the market near the harbour and take supplies to the town, which was still largely confined inside its walls. Up until the beginning of the 18th century, there was little on either side of the track but fields and pastures as far as the eye could see, and faint evidence of human activity. Directly to the south of the road were the harbour, the civil and military administration, and the major religious and commercial institutions; at the other end was the archetypal French-Canadian rural parish. Between the two, Chemin de Saint-Laurent acted as a sort of umbilical cord, an unavoidable thoroughfare and a buffer between different social functions. This historical vocation was vitally important and would be assumed on an even larger scale by the future Saint-Laurent Boulevard.

Chemin de Saint-Laurent would doubtless never have acquired such symbolic importance in the Montréal landscape were it not for the desire of the designers of the fortified town to limit urban growth outside the defensive perimeter in the early 18th century. The authorities long resisted the growth of a second community outside the fortifications, judging that it would be indefensible in case of attack. Up until 1725, Montréal fit the model of a European-style stronghold relatively well, with 90% of its inhabitants living inside the walls. In the first third of that century, the town's population stabilized at about 3,000 souls, with a permanent garrison of 250 soldiers.

By the 18th century, the town confined within the fortifications could no longer resist the lure of the near-limitless virgin expanses of North America outside its walls, and would outgrow Chaussegros de Léry's urban plans. As might be expected in a community subject to such strict social and spatial controls, the system would spring a leak in about 1730 at the most suitable point for expanding into the outlying countryside, ripe for colonization and exploitation—along the future Saint-Laurent Boulevard. Thanks to this phenomenon, Mont-

réal would become a town in its own right for the first time and a site of independent development, no longer merely a keystone in a continental route ruled by the needs of the French mercantile empire. Even back then, the urban landscape of Montréal as it would appear in the following century had been largely determined.

A Suburb Appears Outside the Walls

In fact, by the mid-18th century, three satellite settlements were gradually taking shape around the outside of the fortifications, including the Faubourg Saint-Laurent, just to the north, Sainte-Marie to the east (which would become the *Faubourg à la mélasse* a century later) and Saint-Joseph, the future Griffintown, to the west. The concessions granted along Chemin de Saint-Laurent are clearly visible, for instance, on the map drawn in 1767 by surveyor Paul Jourdain dit Labrosse, and are typical of emerging urban development. At that time, the northern suburb had the brightest future of the three expanding outside the walls. While the growth of the eastern and western suburbs along the banks of the St. Lawrence and the future Lachine Canal was limited by geographic constraints, there was no major obstacle impeding Chemin de Saint-Laurent. Its triumphant northward expansion would give Montréal a characteristic upside-down "T" shape for many decades.

By the end of the French regime there were no longer any inexpensive building lots to be had within the walls of Montréal. This property market and the bylaws adopted to prevent fires, in particular the requirement that walls be made of stone, forced the numerous artisans in the town to seek somewhere to live and set up shop outside the fortifications instead.[1] The geographic

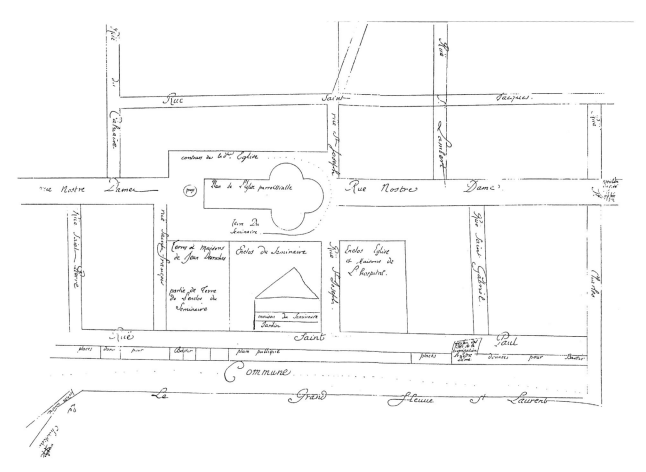

**PLAN OF VILLE-MARIE AND THE FIRST STREETS PLANNED
FOR THE "UPPER TOWN," FRANÇOIS DOLLIER DE CASSON, 1672**

Along with a small group of colonists, Maisonneuve founded the first settlement on the Island of Montréal in spring 1642. He and his followers were supported by a religious organization, the Société de Notre-Dame de Montréal, that had utopian plans of converting Natives and establishing a society of the faithful in Canada. Events confirmed their farsightedness and the outpost, strategically located as it was on the fur trade route, flourished and grew.

The Société de Notre-Dame bankrupted itself in the venture, however, and in 1663 it ceded the Island of Montréal to the Sulpicians, the religious order that had seen to the spiritual needs of the young colony since 1657. As soon as they became the seigneurs of Montréal, the Sulpicians set to work imposing physical order on the town and building some essential institutions. This can be seen in the plan of Montréal streets drawn by Dollier de Casson, the congregation's superior, in 1672. On it can be seen a little street named Saint-Lambert—whose route the future Saint-Laurent Boulevard would follow almost exactly.

A VIEW OF THE CITY OF MONTREAL, JAMES PEACHEY, 1784

This watercolour by Peachey gives us a very good idea of what one would have seen looking south from Mount Royal. At the foot of the walls, a little suburb was gradually taking shape, although at this point it looked a bit lost amidst the vast and peaceful pastoral landscape. Somewhere in the midst of this farmland ran Chemin de Saint-Laurent, completely surrounded by cropland or pastures only a few hundred metres after emerging from the walls.

axis along which these new forces in the city expanded ran along the rural road that was the only way of crossing the island from south to north: Chemin de Saint-Laurent. For the first time, albeit on a small scale, Montrealers had open to them a limitless space that broke completely with the image that had prevailed up to that point, of an agglomeration tightly confined by fortifications, a symbol of both imposed physical constraints and state control. Access for settlement purposes to the farmland just north of the Saint-Martin creek meant that the idea of "North American-ness" had clearly forced its way into the way Montréal was viewed.

The outward expansion from the town represented by the granting of lots in 1730 along the southern portion of Chemin de Saint-Laurent also spelled the end for the state-controlled mercantilism imposed by the French Crown in Montréal. In future, the economic development of the town and the entire region would lie in the hands of entrepreneurs, removed from the privileges conferred by close association with the powers that be within the fortified walls. In this sense, access to the "open" lands north of the town already meant that entrepreneurs were free to conduct their business, to move about as they wished and to engage in activities that might well overthrow the economic power of the ancien Régime, in the long run—and to do so for their personal profit. The unbounded expanses accessible from Chemin de Saint-Laurent would make the town's fortune in the coming century, as new forms of trade and production would take over from merely collecting furs, military logistics and missionary endeavours. In the mid-18th century, however, this important innovation was still widely seen as a marginal development.

Up to the end of the French regime, in 1760, the Montréal economy remained entirely dependent on exports of raw materials to the Old World. The situation changed when Chemin de Saint-Laurent grew out of its role as a mere thoroughfare to become a site of artisanal and, gradually, industrial production. As early as 1781, there were already more homes in the suburbs than in the town proper. The idea of added value, which began to play a part in trade in the late 18th century, was not restricted to the northern suburb; but the Faubourg Saint-Laurent embodied the essence of this concept very well, for it sat pressed up against the town, and residents did not have far to go to reach their main market, Montréal. During this time, the population of greater Montréal grew to 9,000 by 1805, with two-thirds of this number living outside the walls. A new social reality had arrived, heralding a new vocation for the Saint-Laurent corridor and, with it, for the town as a whole:

" With the natural increase in population in the Montréal region and the arrival of new immigrants, new opportunities presented themselves, not only for the merchant community that began to shift its attention from the fur trade to the general country trade, but also for local artisans producing a variety of consumer goods from candles to shoes, from chairs to agricultural implements.[2] "

From Chemin de Saint-Laurent to Saint-Laurent Boulevard

In 1801, the town authorities voted to tear down the fortifications, which were no longer of any importance in the city's social development. The old walls were not only falling apart, but represented a serious hindrance to the movement of people and goods in and around greater Montréal. The decision in itself confirmed a new economic approach, in which territory was not just something to be travelled through and defended, but also to be occupied and developed through the new-found tools offered by capitalism. Emerging industrial technology was accompanied by a new division of labour, reflected in Montréal by the suburbs' specialization in highly specific fields of activity:

"During the period of demolition the city experienced the beginning of a swell of immigration from Europe following the Napoleonic wars, as well as the beginning of the Industrial Revolution in Canada with the introduction of steam power. The economic differentiation that had developed over the course of the 18th century between the town as a commercial and business centre and the faubourgs or suburbs as places of production intensified.[3] "

While people were still only contemplating the demolition of the fortifications designed by Chaussegros de Léry, in 1801 surveyor and architect Louis Charland prepared a legal document and a drawing describing with great precision the location and size of the various buildings that had recently gone up on Chemin de Saint-Laurent, from the gate of the same name to what is now Sainte-Catherine Street. At the time, the road already had all the trappings of an urban street lined with homes, many of them two-storey structures. This notarial document, with so much architectural detail, was drawn up to validate construction work by the town to provide Chemin de Saint-Laurent with its first aqueduct. The disappearance of the walls built by the French would greatly accelerate the growth of the suburbs, still modest in size, that were pressing up against the town

gates, and free the Saint-Laurent route of historical obstacles, opening it up to social innovations:

"[Trans] Unlike the town itself, which since 1672 had had a street grid to guide its development, the suburbs expanded with no overall plan but simply as individual landowners saw fit. They were free to divide up their land as they wished, without worrying too much about what the neighbours thought.[4] "

In 1792, to mark out the space that the town would occupy as soon as it was freed from its stone corset, English authorities extended the Montréal town limits by up to 100 chains (2,012 metres) from the fortifications, or to about where Duluth Street now runs. At the same time it was decided to make Chemin de Saint-Laurent the administrative dividing line between the east and west districts of the municipality, foreshadowing the role it would play throughout the modern period as a breakpoint between very different social and cultural realities within Montréal. The space defined in this way was crossed from south to north only by Chemin de Saint-Laurent and hindered by no particular natural obstacles. It would gradually experience a phenomenon unknown up to that point, and which would make Montréal's fortune: land speculation and uncontrolled urban sprawl. When surveyor John Adams published his plan of the town and suburbs in 1825, three out of four Montrealers lived outside Old Montréal, properly speaking, and the rent in the urban fabric caused by the walls had completely disappeared. On his map, Saint-Laurent is considered a street and is named *Main Street*. Its importance is confirmed by the fact that in 1840, it became one of the toll roads in the Montréal region managed by the toll roads commission and at the time was the most heavily

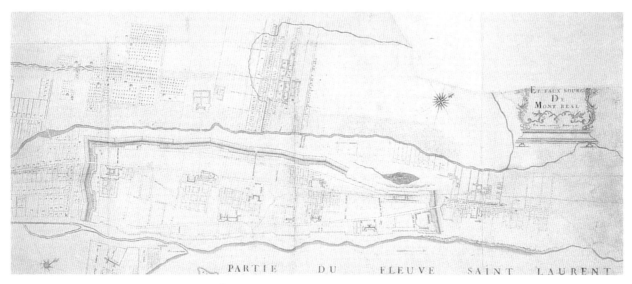

PLAN OF THE TOWN AND SUBURBS OF MONTRÉAL, PAUL JOURDAIN DIT LABROSSE, 1767
A suburb appeared in the mid-18th century, running along Chemin de Saint-Laurent,
north of the swampy Saint-Martin creek. It was less expensive to build wooden houses
outside the walls, and traffic along this single thoroughfare attracted artisans and
workers, keen to live near the town. The Saint-Laurent suburb, clearly visible on this map
dating from 1767, was one of the earliest signs of urban growth at a time when most
Montrealers still lived inside the fortifications.

travelled of the eight roads administered by the commission.[5]

The Main would take its contemporary form at the dawn of the 20th century, after a few twists and turns. The artery, which many real-estate promoters found irresistible and which whipped up both Francophone and Anglophone nationalist fervour, was to be the focus of a number of grandiose plans, but many of them never materialized. The municipality also took an interest in the Main and, in 1890, decided to demolish the whole west side, from Saint-Jacques Street to Roy Street, on the pretext of installing electrical wires and new tramway tracks. In actual fact, it was the marginal inhabitants and the nascent criminality in the neighbourhood that

the authorities wished to nip in the bud. This was when the idea of a wide, elegant avenue first took root in the public imagination.

In 1894, a Boulevard de l'Opéra was proposed. It was to start on the east side of the city and end at the newly built Monument national, highlighting the role of this French-Canadian cultural beacon. The idea was stillborn, however, as was the proposal for a 2,500-seat hall in the Baxter Block, located near the corner of Pine Avenue, and which would have housed the very English Music Academy. Failing a New York-style Fifth Avenue or a replica of the Champs-Élysées, the City Council decided in 1905 to give St. Lawrence Street official status as a "Boulevard." Wishing to open up the artery

MONTREAL FROM MOUNT ROYAL, THOMAS DAVIES, LATE 18TH CENTURY

A British officer-artist, Davies painted this work in 1812 from sketches made in Montréal prior to 1790, when he was last in Canada. The gaping opening of the large Saint-Laurent gate can be seen even from the top of the mountain. At this time, in the late 18th century, the fortifications surrounding the town were still relatively intact and considerably hindered the movement of people and goods in peacetime. Part of Chemin de Saint-Laurent can be seen at the foot of the gate, as it runs through the suburb of the same name.

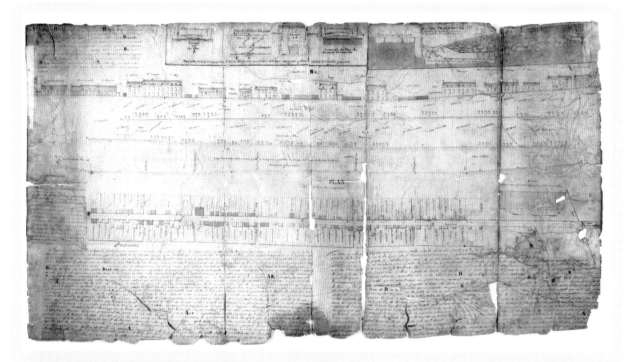

**PLAN OF THE PROPOSED CONSTRUCTION WORK ALONG SAINT-LAURENT STREET
TO IMPROVE SURFACE DRAINAGE, SEPTEMBER 3, 1801, LOUIS CHARLAND**

When Louis Charland came on the scene, the days when private property owners were responsible for maintaining roads and streets on the Island of Montréal were drawing to a close. In 1799, the House of Assembly of Lower Canada adopted legislation calling for the appointment of an inspector in Québec and in Montréal. Charland, born in Québec in 1772, trained at the Petit séminaire de Québec and licensed as a surveyor in 1795, was the first to be appointed to the position in Montréal, in 1799. He was responsible for maintaining roads, streets and bridges and for recruiting the necessary workers. As a government official, militia officer, cartographer and accomplished draftsman, in the course of his career Charland signed many legal documents identifying property lines both on and off the Island of Montréal.

It was in this capacity that he made this drawing in 1801, a sort of first snapshot of the future Main. This seems to have been the first regulated road and sewer work, with Charland's document referring to both the legal agreement binding the property owners and the town and the type of trenching required. Probably intending to describe the scope and exact location of the work for accounting purposes, the surveyor carefully showed the facades and dimensions of the buildings on only one side of the street. We can see that it was already a major artery, lined with stone houses, some of them more than one storey tall, which must have even then played an important role in the town. ◆

all the way down to the River and the docks, the source of economic prosperity, in 1912 the city demolished some of the properties in Old Montréal belonging to the Sisters of the Congregation of Notre-Dame, including a chapel dating back to 1718, known as Notre-Dame-de-Pitié. For the first time, St. Lawrence Boulevard, as it was known to Anglophones, stretched right across the island from one side to the other.

BOULEVARD DE L'OPÉRA, LATE 19TH CENTURY
A sketch by Georges Delfosse shows the famous Boulevard de l'Opéra that was intended to run from the eastern side of the city to the Main and the newly built Monument national. The project was probably too rich for Montrealers' pocketbooks, and it never materialized.

NOTRE-DAME-DE-LA-PITIÉ CHAPEL AND THE GARDEN OF THE SISTERS OF NOTRE-DAME, CIRCA 1885
This convent church, built between 1856 and 1860 to plans by Victor Bourgeau, was expropriated by the city and demolished in 1912 to allow it to extend St. Lawrence Boulevard to De la Commune Street and facilitate access to the port. The photo clearly shows the extensive institutional religious heritage remaining within the old town up to the dawn of the 20th century.

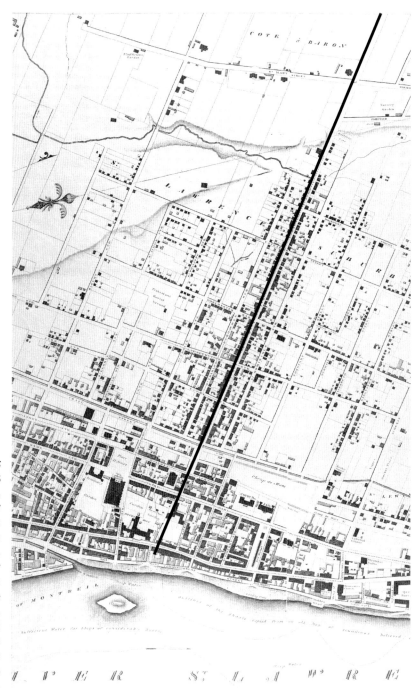

MAP OF THE CITY AND SUBURBS OF MONTREAL, JOHN ADAMS, 1825
When John Adams published this map, the fortification walls had completely disappeared from Montréal's urban landscape and hardly a trace of them can be seen in the street grid shown here. Chemin de Saint-Laurent, on the other hand, had grown by leaps and bounds, in the space of a few years becoming the town's main artery for north-south traffic. Soon, if they had not already started doing so, English-speaking Montrealers would call it the Main, for "Main Street"—reflecting its importance to trade and business in general.

THE BAXTER BLOCK, ABOUT 1918
This Romanesque Revival complex extending from Prince Arthur to Guilbault
streets was very ambitious for its day. It was to have held a 2,500-seat theatre,
but that plan was never carried out.

CHAPTER I

Boulevard of the Industrial Revolution

THE ECONOMIC DEVELOPMENT OF THE NEARBY TOWN BROUGHT
CHANGES IN THE STRICTLY RURAL CHARACTER OF THE MAIN. INITIALLY,
IT WAS ARTISANS AND SHOPKEEPERS WHO SET UP THERE.
AFTER 1880, LARGE FACTORIES ARRIVED, MAKING THE ARTERY
ONE OF CANADA'S BUSIEST MANUFACTURING CENTRES.

FROM VILLAGE TO TOWNS

The transformation of the Saint-Laurent axis from a country road leading inland into an urban artery occurred gradually during the first half of the 19th century, and then with breathtaking speed after the 1880s. The first steps in this direction were taken by humble craftspeople, who formed "urban" villages at the intersection of major arteries, for instance where Chemin de Saint-Laurent met Côte-de-la-Visitation, what is now Mont-Royal Avenue. In the early 19th century, a little community appeared in this district, known then as the Tanneries-des-Bélair, numbering all of 116 souls at the time of the census conducted by Viger in 1825. The inhabitants were mainly engaged in farming, still the dominant activity on Montréal Island, but some of them were shopkeepers, labourers and self-employed workers. At the same time, quarries were being worked just to the west of this district and would provide the grey limestone that would adorn most of Montréal's public buildings in the coming decades.

At the turn of the 19th century, the future Main probably looked like a row of little wooden houses in a semi-rural style. In 1806, the Saint-Laurent suburb as a whole had 514 houses, and a total population of 2,780. Nearly twenty years later, in 1825, the number of buildings had risen to 945, and the population to 6,645.[1] A few of the businesses, shops and industries that would later fuel the tremendous growth of the neighbourhood were already present at this time. For the moment,

Left page:
FEMALE EMPLOYEES OF THE BILTMORE SHIRT CO. LTD. AT WORK IN THE BALFOUR BUILDING, IN THE MID-1930S
Hundreds of women produced shirts on one whole floor of the Balfour Building, at 3575 St. Lawrence Boulevard.

VIEW OF THE MILE END, 1831. This watercolour by James Duncan shows the unobstructed view of Montréal enjoyed by residents of the Mile End. The work was probably commissioned by John Samuel McCord, wishing to preserve a visual record before the rural landscapes of the rapidly growing city were permanently altered. Note the spire of the Anglican Christ Church in the distance, erected on Notre-Dame Street east of Place d'Armes in 1814; it no longer exists.

PROTESTANT AND CATHOLIC CHURCHES IN MONTREAL NEAR THE MOLSON HOUSE, JULY 1840 This painting by Philip John Bainbridge (1817-1881) shows very clearly just how the Molson house still dominated the top of the hill leading up to Sherbrooke Street in the mid-19th century, and how the future boulevard was no more than a track leading inland.

their location and activities were centred less on agriculture as such than on the processing of raw materials from outlying areas. Services were also gradually appearing in these new suburbs, responding to needs arising from the proximity of the "big city," including lodging, restaurants and other services related directly to road transportation. At the same time, wealthy city-dwellers were gradually leaving the lower town, where their social class had traditionally been concentrated, to seek more peaceful surroundings on the heights of Plateau Mont-Royal. The Molson family, for instance, purchased a magnificent villa at the corner of Sherbrooke and Saint-Laurent streets in the 1830s. A huge fire in 1852 in the Saint-Laurent and Québec suburbs would give impetus to this northward flight by wealthy Montrealers.

PLATEAU-MONT-ROYAL, THE FIRST SUBURB

It was in the second half of the 19th century, however, that urban development truly came to the street, when several village municipalities were incorporated on Plateau Mont-Royal, and landowners divided up their agricultural properties for sale to newcomers. The division of the land into lots and promotion by property developers would encourage new uses for the land, which up until then had served essentially for food production. The urbanization of Plateau Mont-Royal took place within the established structure of pre-industrial, rural society; the Plateau gradu-

ST. LAWRENCE STREET IN THE EARLY DAYS OF PHOTOGRAPHY
This shot was taken in about 1860, just north of the future Mont-Royal Avenue. At the time, the street was essentially a link between the city and the countryside, and few people lived on what would later be Plateau Mont-Royal. The transition between the two worlds can be clearly seen, in fact, from the markedly rural style of the wooden houses. On the right of the photo, a hotel operated by A. Patenaude provided lodging for travellers, while a craftsman offered to stable the horses, on the left. On the west side of the street, the wire strung between the poles was only for telegraph communications.

ally became part of the town without actually abandoning the traditions and skills of the past. In fact, it was old families from France, owners of the surrounding farms for many generations and aspiring to some upward social mobility, who were the first to offer their land for residential development.

In this pre-industrial period of the 19th century, two major waves of migration were having an impact on Montréal and consequently on the Main itself. Large numbers of Anglophones were arriving from the British Isles, while at the same time many French Canadians were being drawn from the surrounding countryside by the economic promise of Montréal. The two groups shared the

THE TORRANCE VILLA, OWNED BY THE MOLSON FAMILY
For many years a princely cut-stone home stood on the northwest corner of the Main and Sherbrooke Street, the first of its kind outside the walls of the town. It was built in 1818 by a shipbuilder named Thomas Torrance, who was also an importer of foodstuffs, tea and alcohol. From its doorway one had a remarkable view of the old town and the St. Lawrence River. Brewer and businessman John Molson Sr. (1763-1836) acquired the residence in 1825 to raise his children there, and it remained in his family's hands until about 1910. It was demolished around 1930 to make way for a service station. ◆

THE WEST SIDE OF ST. LAWRENCE STREET IN 1884, NORTH OF VIGER
Lined by buildings often from another age, the Main was gradually entering the industrial era. The street would long bear the marks of its rural heritage, though, in particular the low buildings with their sloped roofs, which changing times would see converted into stores or workshops. By the late 19th century, the Main was already home to hotels and taverns, signs of its future vocation. No fewer than three hotels can be seen in this photo: from left to right, there are the Auberge du Boulevard, the Lion Hotel and the Old Glasgow Hotel.

same urban neighbourhoods and the new villages appearing around Montréal, including those along the Main. The Irish community made its mark in the city, in particular near today's Jean-Talon Street, where its members gathered to play outdoor sports and established social clubs—indeed, there is still a Shamrock Street in the neighbourhood. By 1871, 67% of residents of the Saint-Laurent neighbourhood hailed from the United Kingdom, while Saint-Louis was made up mostly of French Canadians. Right up to the turn of the 20th century, Francophones and Anglophones formed distinct communities side by side on Plateau Mont-

Royal, creating the perception that the Main was also a linguistic dividing line in the city. In 1901, however, the population of Saint-Jean-Baptiste was 85% French Canadian and that of Saint-Louis du Mile-End, 82% French-speaking. This wave of migration was due largely to the efforts of a number of notables, with pedigrees extending back to the French regime, who early on saw the urban development potential of the Main.

A PROPERTY DEVELOPER'S DREAM

Denis-Benjamin Viger, Montréal's first mayor from 1833 to 1836, was one of the first to foresee the urban development that would occur along Saint-Laurent in the late 19th century. In 1861, he left a number of properties in the Lambert Closse fief, in the heart of the village of Saint-Jean-Baptiste, to his cousin Séraphin Cherrier. They would be divided up into lots in 1869. At the same time, two public squares on the Main were created—the marketplace on the corner of Rachel Street, with a very promising future, and what is now Parc du Portugal. The adjacent farmland on the east, owned by Cadieux de Courville, would be split up starting in 1840. Saint-Jean-Baptiste became even more developed in 1872, when the land immediately to the east, the Comte farm, was divided up by promoters Ferdinand David, Sévère Rivard, Michel Laurent and Gustave-Adolphe Drolet. In the space of a few months, 1,200 residential lots were put up for sale, launching the shift to urban development. Indeed, the streets of the emerging Plateau Mont-Royal neighbourhood would often be named for these first large landowners.

In this way the farmland parallel to Chemin de Saint-Laurent, and generally extending in narrow strips from Sherbrooke Street up to Mont-Royal Street, was divided up for urban settlement. The new owners would move in on either side of the Main, beginning with Clark and Saint-Dominique Streets and then pushing the edges of the farmland back to the east and west in the shape of an uneven checkerboard. This approach to development would have a lasting effect on the emerging neighbourhood, for it reproduced the rural social world in an urban setting, and would influence the way future city-dwellers saw themselves. Until quite recently, in fact, they were strongly inclined to be attached to their "villages" and corresponding parishes. It was not until the turn of the 20th century that all the lots available on Plateau Mont-Royal were finally occupied, creating for the first time an urban habitat with no obvious discontinuities. As a result the street

**SAINT-ENFANT-JÉSUS
DU MILE END CHURCH**
This church, first built in 1857-58 and adorned with an Italian Baroque façade in 1901-02, was one of the first to be built outside the walls. For several decades it was one of the nuclei for urban development on Plateau Mont-Royal.

grid in the neighbourhood around Saint-Laurent Boulevard south of Jean-Talon still mirrors the original rural cadastral plan, giving the blocks of houses that very long, narrow rectangular shape unique to urban Montréal.

Although these 19th-century promoters went about their business almost untroubled by public authorities, they were nonetheless influenced by the cultural beliefs and historical heritage of rural Quebec. The social cohesion embodied in this long-established heritage guaranteed that the emerging urban neighbourhood would be organized and develop at a pace in keeping with past practices, particularly the institutional Francophone heritage of Montréal Island. The first traces of this phenomenon were evident as far back as 1846, when all the land between Papineau road and Côte-des-Neiges road was formed into a municipality named Coteau Saint-Louis. The new territorial entity was bordered to the north by Côte Saint-Laurent and the future municipality of the same name, and to the south by the boundary set in 1792 for the town of Montréal. The geographic heart of this territory was on the site of today's Saint-Enfant-Jésus church, on Saint-Dominique Street, just to the north of Saint-Joseph Boulevard. In 1864, a horse-drawn tramway ran up the Main to present-day Mont-Royal Avenue, giving easy access to an area located outside the official city limits.

THE MUNICIPALITY OF SAINT-LOUIS DU MILE-END

The urban development process continued in 1861, when the village of Saint-Jean-Baptiste split off from the southern part of Coteau Saint-Louis. It was bordered on the west by the modern-day Avenue de l'Esplanade, on the east by Papineau and on the north by Mont-Royal Avenue. Development in the municipality was centred around two poles: the Saint-Jean-Baptiste market[2] at the corner of Rachel and the Main, and what is now the Saint-Jean-Baptiste church at the corner of Rachel and Drolet. The village became a town in 1884, when it had 8,000 inhabitants within its boundaries. It was annexed by Montréal in 1886, however, during the first major wave of expansion by the city. Over the decades, these early settlements attracted the basic religious, economic and administrative institutions required to establish and, later, manage the new suburbs to the north of Montréal. Even today, the neighbourhoods extending on either side of Saint-Laurent Boulevard are often centred on public squares and buildings dating back more than 100 years.

SAINT-JEAN-BAPTISTE MARKET, CIRCA 1930
The Saint-Jean-Baptiste market, established in 1908 on the northeast corner of Rachel Street, was full of growers' and merchants' stalls right up until 1966. As such, it was an important factor in the development of this part of the Main. The building in the photo was the first to be built on the site, where the Parc des Amériques is now located.

In 1878, at almost the same time as the City of Montréal was swallowing up the village of Saint-Jean-Baptiste, a new community known as the Village de Saint-Louis du Mile-End[3] was born just to the north. It was bordered on the east by what is now Henri-Julien Street, on the west by Hutchison Street and the Municipality of Outremont, itself created in 1875, and on the north by the railway line running alongside Van Horne Street. In reality, the village was created largely because St. Lawrence Boulevard crossed it from north to south and formed its

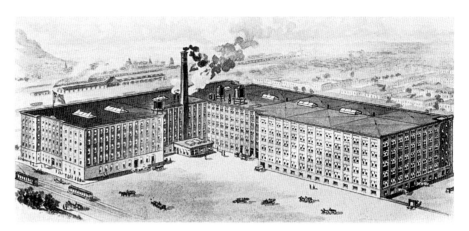

THE PECK FACTORY, CIRCA 1915
The building erected by John W. Peck & Co., still standing at the corner of Saint-Viateur and the Main, shows how garment manufacturers flocked to inexpensive suburban land in the early 20th century—in this case, the municipality of Saint-Louis du Mile-End. In its day, the Peck factory was the second largest on Montréal Island.

TOWN HALL OF THE MUNICIPALITY OF SAINT-LOUIS DU MILE-END
The Gothic Revival building, built in 1905-08, housed a police station, a fire hall and the municipal council chambers.

economic backbone. At the time when this new civil entity appeared, Plateau Mont-Royal was experiencing a veritable population explosion, and a wave of urbanization was spreading throughout this part of the island. In 1891, Saint-Louis du Mile-End numbered 3,449 citizens, many of them stonemasons or labourers, often unskilled, hired by small, locally oriented businesses.

Barely more than 15 years later, in 1908, it had grown into a sizeable municipality with a total population of 25,000. Nearly 25 factories had sprung up, mainly in the garment and textile industries, and they alone employed some 5,000 people. The goods produced by the highly mechanized factories lining the Main were shipped across Canada. In fact, Saint-Louis du Mile-End appeared so prosperous that it whetted Montréal's appetite, and the city annexed it in 1910, turning it into the Laurier district. In the space of just one generation, the new suburbs had exceeded their promoters' expectations and created some of the country's most vibrant economic and urban entities.

LAYING TRAMWAY TRACKS AT THE CORNER OF CRAIG AND ST. LAWRENCE STREETS, 1893
The introduction of electrically operated tramways in 1892 would be a major innovation on the Main. With its larger and faster vehicles, this type of urban transit would make it possible to move workers over greater distances, encouraging urban sprawl. The photo shows how the tramway required major investments in infrastructure and brutally transformed the visual and sound environment on the Main. This time, there was no doubt that industrialization had arrived to stay.

BIRTH OF A MASS URBAN CULTURE

The urbanization of Chemin de Saint-Laurent was very much a part of the massive social transformations affecting Canada and, indeed, all of North America, starting in the mid-19th century. For many new residents of the villages of Saint-Jean-Baptiste and Saint-Louis du Mile-End, this was their first experience of new forms of social organization—working for wages, specialization, and industrial production methods. In this urban enclave, having left the countryside behind them, they now found that they had to devote most of their time to working in a shop or factory. Tied to repetitive industrial jobs all year long, often for more than

THE MAIN AT THE CORNER OF CRAIG, CIRCA 1910
There is nothing left of this block of houses that once stood on the northeast corner of Craig Street (now Saint-Antoine). The site is now occupied by a parking lot for the Courthouse and by the Ville-Marie expressway.

60 hours a week, they no longer had the time to see to all their own material needs. As a result, they became consumers of manufactured goods, from clothing to furniture and household items.

Soon, this growing demand convinced new entrepreneurs to launch their own businesses. They, too, required factory manpower, and this led to calls to boost the population of the working-class neighbourhoods around the Main. In 1880, for instance, 37,000 Montrealers were employed as factory workers. By 1911 this total had risen to 61,000, and by 1921 it had rocketed to 119,000.[4] The fact that a continuously growing throng of people were leaving behind the old farms and artisanal production and throwing themselves into the industrial era tended to lead to uniformity not only in the type of goods available on the market, but also in attitudes and forms of social organization. Rather than an older mercantile economy based on producers widely dispersed across a vast territory, by the mid-19th century there tended to be urban nuclei where everyone was subject to the same working conditions.

“ [Trans] The fundamental transformation that occurred in the 19th century, industrialization, changed the very nature of the city, altering its economic roles, the composition of its population and its social relationships...[5] ”

FOGARTY SHOE FACTORY AND SHOP, 1871
This print by Eugene Haberer gives a good idea of the type of industry that set up on the Main in the late 19th century, before new electrically powered production processes made garment manufacturing the key industry. This factory was located on the southeast corner of St. Lawrence and St. Catherine streets. A horse-drawn trolley can also be seen, evidence that the Montreal City Passenger Railway Company had been offering public transit service on wooden tracks along the Main since 1861. Note that the artist intentionally reduced the size of the figures and horses to make the building appear more imposing. ◆

This metamorphosis was reflected tangibly in the plan of the city, its expansion, and the emerging social division of the urban space.

Heavily industrialized areas such as the Main were, after 1880, the Canadian birthplace of a mass culture, the result of the fact that the vast majority of workers were involved in a single type of production. Because they all earned much the same wages, had access at the same time to very similar products and lived in the same part of the city, factory workers ended up forming a social class unto themselves. Throughout this period they also suffered increasing poverty, due to the sharp ups and downs in the economy, the often seasonal nature of their work and systematic exploitation by their employers. Montréal was Canada's leading manufacturing centre in the early 20th century, with factories spread along three separate axes: westward on the banks of the Lachine Canal, eastward through the Sainte-Marie and Hochelaga neighbourhoods and the town of Maisonneuve, and northward along St. Lawrence Boulevard. While factories in the first two industrial districts produced iron, steel, textile and transportation equipment, along with shoes and food products, businesses along the Main specialized in consumer goods, mostly clothing, but also tobacco, beer and printing.

Montréal was Canada's leading manufacturing centre in the early 20th century, with factories spread along three separate axes: westward on the banks of the Lachine Canal, eastward through the Sainte-Marie and Hochelaga neighbourhoods and the town of Maisonneuve, and northward along St. Lawrence Boulevard.

When Clothing Was King

Most of the workers in the towns, it must be understood, no longer had the time to make their own clothing nor the financial means to have tailors or other skilled craftsmen make it for them. Since their budgets were limited, urban workers turned to factory-produced clothing offering the twofold advantage of great quantity and unbeatable prices. The appearance of this new branch of the industry along the Main in about 1900 brought even more extensive changes to a neighbourhood that was already being transformed. In 1870, 90% of menswear produced in Montréal was made by artisanal tailors. By 1898, nearly 30 years later, this percentage had fallen to 34%. All across Canada, this type of production was suffering the same fate, as the proportion of men's clothing produced in factories rose from 51% in 1901 to between 80% and 90% by 1905.[6] Womenswear followed much the same trend, so much so that by 1921 the garment trade had become the leading industry in greater Montréal. That year, fully one-quarter of all workers in the city were employed in garment factories.[7]

THE BILTMORE SHIRT CO. LTD. LAUNDRY, 3575 ST. LAWRENCE

In the mid-1930s, the Balfour Building, at the corner of Prince-Arthur, was a bustling place, with thousands of women at work. In this photo, they are busy ironing, folding and boxing shirts for shipping.

At the dawn of the 20th century, the garment industry very quickly came to dominate the neighbourhood surrounding the intersection of Sainte-Catherine and Bleury. North of Sherbrooke, in a long line stretching up St. Lawrence Boulevard to Bernard Street, garment factories, some of them up to ten storeys high, dominated the cityscape

At the dawn of the 20th century, the garment industry very quickly came to dominate the neighbourhood surrounding the intersection of Sainte-Catherine and Bleury. North of Sherbrooke, in a long line stretching up St. Lawrence Boulevard to Bernard Street, garment factories, some of them up to ten storeys high, dominated the cityscape. There, in the largest concentration of garment factories in 1920s Canada, thousands of people toiled under often pitiful conditions. Access to inexpensive ready-to-wear clothing for both men and women meant sweeping changes in behaviour and new lifestyles, and in fact accelerated the growth of a mass culture among the lower classes. Tastes, fashion trends and marketing brought widespread changes to the garment trade, which had to constantly adjust and come up with new products. In a single generation, the Main completely reshaped the wardrobes of the lower and middle classes in Canada:

“ By the 1930s clothing production in the women's wear industry included a large variety of products: coats, suits and skirts, dresses and blouses, children's wear, undergarments, sportswear, rainwear, kimonos and a large number of other products as well. The men's and boy's industry included traditional men's suits and coats, separate coats, trousers, smoking jackets, and rainwear; the work clothes sector of the industry produced uniforms, overalls, work pants and shirts, work coats and jumpers. In addition to these main areas of manufacture, men's furnishings (collars and cuffs), caps and hats, and a separate branch for shirts and children's blouses were all in production by the mid-1920s.[8] ”

GROWING SOCIAL UNREST

The impact of the garment factories on the Main, like everywhere else, was more than economic. The emergence of new production processes also sparked new social ideas, previously unheard of and often revolutionary for the time. The garment industry had created a sizeable proletariat in just a few years, most of them living under difficult economic conditions, and would be the scene of bitter social conflicts in the early years of the 20th century. Throughout this period, the area around St. Lawrence Boulevard, in particular, found itself in the forefront of the national trade union and protest movements. For instance, the first May Day

A PICKET LINE, CIRCA 1960
Amalgamated Clothing Workers of America strikers wave signs in
different languages on the picket line outside a clothing factory.

parade to be held in Montréal was on the Main in 1906, at a time when this type
of demonstration was considered a threat to the established order. Hirsch
Hershman, an eyewitness, left us this description:

> ❝[Trans] The whole winter had been spent thinking about and planning dif-
> ferent options for this May Day celebration (1906). All the Jewish unions and
> most of those with a mainly Christian membership had sent delegates to the
> meetings organized for this purpose by the (anarchist) Mutual Aid circle. In
> the end it was decided to down tools that day and to march through the streets
> with red flags all the way to Champ-de-Mars.

(...) Finally, May Day was celebrated magnificently in Montreal. 1,800 workers of all origins set off from Empire Hall at two o'clock in the afternoon, accompanied by an Italian orchestra of twenty trumpeters who knew nothing but *La Marseillaise*. The parade headed for Champ-de-Mars, where enthusiastic speeches were given in all the languages understood by the crowd.[9] ""

A report in *La Presse* the next day also gives a good idea of the speeches and the attitude of the participants:

"" [Trans] About one thousand workers, most of them Jews, Russians and other foreign nationalities, paraded through some of our streets yesterday evening singing *l'Internationale*, the anthem dear to all socialists.

(...) Robert E. Scott, of the workers socialist party, was the standard bearer. Seizing a red flag bearing the words "Workers of the World, Unite," he advanced, trailed by party followers and a number of women.

> The 1937 strike set a precedent not only because emotions ran so high, but also because the strikers made significant gains. It would foreshadow the labour battles of the war years. After 25 days on the picket line, the workers returned to the factory floor with an average wage of $16, a 44-hour week and a union recognized by management.

A DEMONSTRATION DURING A STRIKE BY GARMENT WORKERS, 1937
On April 15, 1937, 5,000 ladies' garment workers went on strike on St. Lawrence Boulevard and in small workshops near St. Catherine Street. Most of them were French-Canadian women, working long hours for little pay. The walkout followed months of groundwork and convincing by the International Ladies' Garment Workers' Union, led by such long-time Jewish unionists as Bernard Shane, Rose Pesotta and Léa Roback.

(...) The associations represented in the procession were the union of industrial workers, the workers socialist party, the federation of Italian socialists and the social democrats.[10] *"*

Beginning in 1900, a wind of social protest began blowing along the Main, more powerful than anything Montréal had known up to that point. Leftist ideologies found there a fertile breeding ground, and were carried throughout Quebec by a union spearhead consisting for the most part of immigrant and Jewish workers. Huge strikes soon broke out in the garment industry. In 1912, for instance, 4,000 workers on St. Lawrence Boulevard, affiliated with the United Garment Workers of America, won the right to a 49-hour week after a nine-week work stoppage. Strikes, often marred by violence, occurred almost every year on the Main, culminating in 1937 when 7,000 women's garment workers, supported by the International Ladies' Garment Workers' Union, took to the streets. Since profit margins in the garment industry were slim and wages very low, businesses in this industry relied heavily on women workers. In 1921, in Montréal, 45% of women factory workers were in the garment trade. By comparison, only 17% of male workers at the time were employed in the garment industry, and most of them were skilled cutters.[11]

A Historic Strike by French-Canadian Women

In many ways, the 1937 strike was emblematic of the social protest movements that rocked St. Lawrence Boulevard in the 20th century. In those days, a large proportion of the unskilled workers in the ladies' wear industry were Francophone women from the surrounding countryside, organized for the first time by a group of experienced Jewish unionists intent on winning a collective agreement. Among the strikers' demands in 1937 were a 44-hour work week, the abolition of work at home, a 20% wage increase and recognition of the union. The strikers were victorious after a mere three weeks, and the 1937 walkout was the turning point in a long evolution that saw Francophones adopt the methods and views of workers as they were being expressed elsewhere in North America. The strike also established the influence on the Main of immigrant communities that had arrived after 1900, in particular Jews from Eastern Europe. This new combination of factory work and mass immigration would give the Main its very special character.

COOPER BUILDING IN 1952
The Cooper Building, devoted entirely to the garment trade, proudly displayed its name. In those days automobile traffic was two-way on the Main, and buses manufactured in Lachine by the Canadian Car company had gradually started replacing the electric trams. No fewer than four Jewish restaurants can be seen on both sides of the street in this photo. In the immediate post-war period, the Main would be swept by a new wave of immigrants that would profoundly transform the neighbourhood's cultural identity.

CHAPTER 2

Boulevard of New Arrivals

THE COMING OF LARGE-SCALE INDUSTRIALIZATION TO THE MAIN
IN THE EARLY 20TH CENTURY OPENED THE CITY AND THE
NEIGHBOURHOOD TO INTERNATIONAL INFLUENCES. FLEEING THE
PERSECUTION AND POVERTY OF THE OLD WORLD, HUNDREDS OF
THOUSANDS OF IMMIGRANTS ARRIVED IN MONTRÉAL AND FLOCKED
TO ST. LAWRENCE BOULEVARD SEEKING LODGING AND WORK.

THE GREAT WAVE OF IMMIGRANTS, 1905-1914

The surge of industrialization that would make Montréal the key producer of household goods in Canada in the late 19th century also had immense demographic repercussions. With the growth in manufacturing in the city came an unprecedented demand for workers, which the local population could not meet in the short term. Montréal manufacturers were supplying a huge and constantly expanding domestic market, one that the Canadian transcontinental railway, opened in 1886, was continuing to broaden. At the same time, in Europe, the same phenomena of urban concentration and worker specialization as a result of mechanization were "freeing" whole communities from their age-old ties to the land and traditional means of production. The combination of these two factors, the rapid growth of new markets in North America and the desire among European peasants to escape political and economic oppression in their homelands, led to an enormous population shift from one continent to the other, which new means of trans-Atlantic transportation finally made possible on a large scale.

In the United States, this human flood from the Old World to the New had truly begun back in the 1880s, at least 20 to 30 years before a similar phenomenon occurred in Canada. Between 1881 and 1890, no fewer than 5.2 million immigrants arrived in the United States, most of them from Eastern and Southern

Left page:
THE MAIN BEFORE THE AGE OF THE AUTOMOBILE
Taken in about 1905, looking south from the corner of St. Catherine, this photo from the Notman Studio shows how St. Lawrence Boulevard was both a commercial artery and a street devoted to entertainment and pleasure. Lower on the Main, a group of passengers prepares to board a first-generation electric tramway.

IMMIGRANTS ARRIVING IN MONTRÉAL, CIRCA 1910
Between 1905 and 1914, the wharves of the Allan shipping company, located right at the foot of St. Lawrence Boulevard, were the welcome mat for hundreds of thousands of newcomers, who spread out from there all across the country. Many of them remained in Montréal, however, where they gradually moved northward up the Main from the port, bringing new cultures and sounds to a rapidly industrializing neighbourhood.

Boulevard Saint-Laurent
Ville de Montréal
Québec

Europe. Between 1901 and 1910, this figure climbed to 8.8 million, still from the same regions—the highest number of immigrants the U.S. ever absorbed in a single decade. In 1910, the 13.5 million immigrants accounted for 14.7% of the total U.S. population.[1] In Canada, the flood of immigrants did not really begin until the turn of the 20th century, encouraged by the government of Wilfrid Laurier, who was intent on settling Western Canada and battling American influence there.

Laurier appointed Clifford Sifton Minister of the Interior in 1896 and made him responsible for designing a policy intended to lure huge numbers of immigrants to Canada. Along with British and American immigrants, Sifton was looking to attract people of hardy stock, who were used to harsh conditions and ready to settle as-yet undeveloped regions.[2] Between 1901 and 1910, close to 1.7 million immigrants crossed Canada's borders. Indeed, by 1911, fully 24.6% of Canada's population was foreign-born. In the subsequent decade, Canada took in another wave of immigrants; most arrived shortly before the First World War broke out in August 1914. Among the newcomers were many Italians, Russians, Ukrainians, Polish and Chinese, most of whom headed for the Canadian West, where they would homestead or work on the railway needed to develop the newly opened lands.

Saint Lawrence Boulevard
City of Montreal
Quebec

JEWISH IMMIGRANTS TOP THE LIST

The massive arrival of new citizens, the largest in Canadian history, also had a marked impact on Montréal's development. Starting in 1880, but especially after 1900, workers from other lands flooded into the port of Montréal. Some of them would remain in the city to work in the garment trade, in the construction of new urban infrastructures and in light industry. Other newcomers rushed to open shops in the burgeoning immigrant communities and even elsewhere in the city. One community in particular stood out—Yiddish-speaking Jews from the western lands of the Russian Empire. Conditions in Eastern Europe were so terrible in the early 20th century that huge numbers of Jews fled their homes and the violent pogroms fomented by the czarist authorities.

THE BETH YEHUDA SYNAGOGUE, CIRCA 1908
The Beth Yehuda synagogue (in the centre of the photo), located on La Gauchetière almost at the corner of the Main, moved into an old theatre with the highly irreverent name of Le Bijou. Recently arrived Jewish immigrants were often obliged to use rather odd premises as places of worship, including shops, newly converted homes and even theatres. So it was that for many years a pious public thronged to the Monument national at the Jewish New Year and the Yom Kippur fast—quite a contrast with the usual light-hearted and fun-filled atmosphere there. ◆

THE EKERS' BREWERY, CIRCA 1910
The Ekers building, just south of Sherbrooke Street, is probably the finest industrial block on the Main. The 1894 Romanesque Revival building was designed by Alexander Francis Dunlop and faced in greystone. An annex was added on the Saint-Norbert side in 1920. Today it houses the Just for Laughs Museum. The photo also shows an electric tramway climbing the steep slope up to Sherbrooke, which had long been a serious obstacle for horse-drawn passenger vehicles.

מיין סטריט
מאנטרעאל
קוויבעק

By 1905, Jews were already Montréal's largest immigrant community. They numbered close to 30,000 in 1911, nearly all of them living along St. Lawrence Boulevard. By 1931, there were just under 60,000. For half a century, until the arrival of a new wave of immigrants after the Second World War, Yiddish was the most widely spoken language in Montréal, after French and English. This does not mean that the Jewish immigrants who arrived in the early 1900s had it easy. An article in *La Patrie*, on January 13, 1905, explained that the Jewish community already established in Montréal had had to take extraordinary steps to help the newcomers:

“[Trans] An important step was taken yesterday to solve the problem of lodging the Russian Jewish immigrants who now number 800 in Montréal.

The Baron de Hirsch Institute emergency committee has rented a spacious building at 950 St. Lawrence Boulevard,[3] with room for 100 people (...) and it is hoped that at least 300 Jews can be accommodated there starting this evening. The goal is not to provide only shelter, but also food and care.

Yesterday, a number of them who had suffered from the cold received medical attention. The emergency committee met from 8 o'clock yesterday morning until 2 o'clock this morning, to respond to the demands of the most needy, and to distribute warm clothing, shoes and overshoes. There has been no appreciable change in the situation as regards finding work for these immigrants.[4]”

A WELL-ORGANIZED PROLETARIAT

In Montréal, as elsewhere in North America in the late 19th century, huge numbers of Jewish immigrants were finding work in the needle trades, where they made up most of the skilled workforce. In 1931, 35% of Jews in greater Montréal were manufacturing workers, and 75% of them earned their living in the textile and garment industries, where they formed a readily identifiable and very well organized proletariat.[5] It must be remembered, in this context, that working conditions in Montréal factories were particularly deplorable. Journalist Israël Medres penned an eloquent description of the conditions in factories along St. Lawrence Boulevard:

“The history of the Jewish workers' movement in Canada began some forty years ago (in 1892) when the garment industries began to grow and the first signs of massive Jewish immigration to Canada appeared.

Some Jewish workers had already managed to settle in Canada several years earlier, in fact, when the clothing industry was still in its infancy, and when the first "home" workshops opened, to make inexpensive clothing. Up to that point, lower-quality clothing had been turned out by seamstresses in their spare time. People with more up-to-date and refined tastes turned to skilled tailors to make their clothes.

SOUVENIR OF A BAR MITZVAH, CIRCA 1900
In this photo taken at the studio of L.V. Côté, on the Main, a young boy wearing a *talit* poses proudly with other family members on his day of coming of age. This type of photo was often sent back to Eastern Europe to show how well yesterday's immigrants had fit into their host society, without abandoning their Jewish traditions.

मांट्रियाल, न्यूयॉर्क
सेंट लॉरां स्ट्रीट

The workers needed for the earliest clothing workshops were recruited from among the immigrants coming off the ships in the port, and immediately sent to work in factories. They laboured for long hours and very little money. Their standard of living was very low, however, and their needs very simple.[6] **"**

THE JEWISH COMMUNITY TAKES SHAPE ON THE MAIN

In 1905, Medres described in his memoirs[7] how the geographic heart of the Jewish community in Montréal was located at the corner of St. Urbain and Dorchester (now René-Lévesque Boulevard), in the neighbourhood located close to the port, where so many newcomers first stepped off the ship. Like other inhabitants of Montréal before them, the Jews soon found the older quarters of the city stifling. They began migrating to the suburbs on the north side of the city shortly after the end of the First World War. In reality, many of them were simply following their work, which was also migrating to Plateau Mont-Royal as factories became electrically powered and mechanized. The huge factories that sprang up along St. Lawrence Boulevard and the large Jewish communities that appeared went hand in hand.

Like many immigrants of the day, the Jews who moved onto the streets around the Main brought with them a strong community spirit. In 1907, for instance, a

HIRSCH WOLOFSKY, CIRCA 1926
Founder of Montréal's main Yiddish daily, the *Keneder Odler* (the Jewish Eagle), Wolofsky had been fascinated as a teenager in Poland by Jewish writing and journalism. He was forced to emigrate by the military conscription imposed on Jews under the Russian empire, and arrived in Montréal in late 1900. At that point there were probably no more than about 5,000 Jews in Montréal, most of them fresh off the boat, like himself. After working in a factory and later operating a grocery on the Main, Wolofsky launched the *Odler* in 1907, fulfilling a lifelong dream. The newspaper came on the scene at a time when there was a real need for something like it to bring together the immigrant Jewish community. The *Odler* was an overnight success, and its editor found himself propelled to the forefront of a quickly growing network of Jewish institutions. Wolofsky's reputation, thanks to his newspaper, gave him access to all the high-profile causes in Montréal, including the creation between the wars of the Canadian Jewish Congress, the United Talmud Torahs and the Jewish General Hospital. Wolofsky also won renown in 1923, when he established the *Va'ad Ha'ir*, an organization responsible for regulating the sale of kosher products. When he died in 1949, there were over 60,000 Jews in Montréal, making them the largest of all the city's immigrant communities. ◆

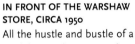

IN FRONT OF THE WARSHAW STORE, CIRCA 1950
All the hustle and bustle of a weekday can be seen in this candid photo. Back in those days Warshaw's did not have the long modern display window it now has, and it was a rather modest-looking little shop. Slightly farther north can be seen the sign for Schwartz's delicatessen. In the background is the dark mass of the Vineberg Building, a garment factory at the time.

THE SHAARE TFILE SYNAGOGUE, BETWEEN 1901 AND 1910
When it was built at the turn of the 20th century on the corner of Milton and Clark, the Shaare Tfile (the gates of prayer) synagogue, also known as the Austro-Hungarian synagogue, was considered a long way away from the Jewish quarter, normally located much farther south. At the time, few immigrants had ventured farther north than Ontario Street, and Sherbrooke Street was considered "uptown." By the 1930s, when most of the Jewish community had moved north of Mont-Royal Avenue, the building was no longer used as a place of worship. In fact, in a fitting turn of events, the completely remodelled synagogue took on a new identity in 1959, as the Cinéma Élysée, which would become one of Montréal's leading movie theatres.

THE PRESSES OF THE *KENEDER ODLER*, CIRCA 1932
To mark its 25th anniversary, in 1932, the *Keneder Odler* devoted a special issue to its achievements—this photo is from that issue. At the time, the newspaper was printed in the basement of 4050 St. Lawrence Boulevard, and the editorial offices were located on the first floor of the same building, just north of Duluth Street.

Yiddish-language daily paper was founded in Montréal by Hirsch Wolofsky, right at the corner of Ontario Street and the Main, helping to bind together emerging Jewish institutions. Yiddish-speaking immigrants adopted a cultural pattern that French Canadians had created before them on these same city blocks, and which the urban cadastral plan devised in the late 19th century greatly simplified. A dense and diverse network of synagogues, charitable organizations, artistic and cultural circles and Jewish trade unions in the garment trade took shape on Plateau

Mont-Royal after 1920, not to mention shops of all kinds, grocers, restaurants and public meeting places. In the space of a few years after the First World War, Yiddish-speakers made the Saint-Louis quarter the centre of immigrant Jewish life in Montréal:

> Two streets below our own came the Main. Rich in delights, but also squalid, filthy, and hollering with stores whose wares, whether furniture or fruit, were ugly or damaged.
>
> The Main, with something for all appetites, was dedicated to pinching pennies from the poor, but it was also there to entertain, educate and comfort us too. Across the street from the synagogue you could see 'the picture they claimed could never be made'. A little further down the street there was the Workmen's Circle and, if you liked, a strip show. Peaches, Margo, Lili St. Cyr. Around the corner, there was the ritual baths, the *shvitz* or *mikva*, where my grandfather and his cronies went before the High Holidays, emerging boiling red from the highest reaches of the steam rooms to happily flog each other with brushes fashioned of pine tree branches. Where supremely orthodox women went once a month to purify themselves.[8]

EMOTIONALLY SIGNIFICANT SPACES

Certain spaces that had been laid out and developed many decades earlier by Francophones or Anglophones soon became emblems in the eyes of Jewish Montrealers and acquired an exceptional emotional significance in their community. Jeanne Mance Park, for example, known at the time as Fletcher's Field, became a favourite meeting place for Yiddish speakers between the wars. Indeed, the green space would be the site of several important community institutions in the 1930s, including the Jewish Public Library, the Mortimer B. Davis sports and cultural centre (Young Men's and Young Women's Hebrew Association) and the Old Folks' Home. It was also the scene of many huge political demonstrations. The same was true of the Mountain, forming a dark and compact mass crowned by its cross, visible from almost every street that intersected with St. Lawrence. Indeed, Montréal made such an impression on the new residents of the neighbourhood that many immigrant poets paid tribute to it in works written in Yiddish or English.

YIDDISH ON THE MAIN, 1958
The Conservative candidates in the federal election on March 31, 1958, appealed to voters in a multitude of languages.

مونتریال
شارع سان لوران
کیاك

Boulevard of New Arrivals • 55

JOSEPH SCHUBERT (1889-1952)

Born in Rumania, Schubert immigrated to Canada in 1903, and was a leading Montréal figure for many years in the garment industry unions and in the Jewish socialist movement. Running for the Workers' Party of Canada, he was elected in 1924 as a municipal councillor in the Saint-Louis district, which took in St. Lawrence Boulevard from Sherbrooke Street up to Mont-Royal Avenue. He championed workers' causes, calling for a class struggle to have ownership of natural resources and means of industrial production restored to them. Schubert was elected over and over again for 16 years, and saw to it that the municipal administration gave workers in his neighbourhood tangible benefits, including public sports facilities, free medical attention and tax cuts for the poor. It was in this spirit that in 1931–32 he had public baths built on the corner of St. Lawrence Street and Bagg Street. The building, which bears his name, was recently renovated. Workers without hot water in their homes would go there to bathe, and their children to play in the swimming pool.

Schubert also fought throughout the 1930s to have the municipality grant its workers an eight-hour day and a minimum wage of 50 cents, not to mention a pension fund. He also fought at City Hall for women's suffrage, for universal pensions at age 65 and for mothers' allowances. Schubert was a very active figure in the International Ladies' Garment Workers' Union and the Conseil du travail du Québec, and helped to found the Co-operative Commonwealth Federation (CCF) in 1933, a coalition of leftist parties on the federal scene. In 1935, Schubert became the first chairman of the Joint Committee of the Men's and Boy's Clothing Industry, an organization that administered collective agreements in the menswear industry. He held the position until his death in 1952. ◆

Schubert Baths in 1932.

Our churchy city becomes even more pious
on Sundays, the golden crosses shine and gleam
while the big bells ring with loud
hallelujahs and the little bells answer
their low amens; the tidy peaceful streets
lie dreaming in broad daylight murmuring
endearments to me who is such a Yiddish Jew
that even in my footsteps they must hear
how the music of my Yiddish song sounds
through the rhythm of my Hebrew prayer.[9]

مانطريال - كيوبك
سينت لوريس ستريت

ITALIAN AND CHINESE IMMIGRANTS ARRIVE

The vibrant Jewish cultural and artistic life on St. Lawrence Boulevard had no equivalent elsewhere in greater Montréal in the period between the wars. Many other communities took root in the neighbourhood during these years, however, including immigrants from Italy, for whom Montréal had become a vitally important hub for those continuing farther inland. The major Canadian railway companies were looking for experienced workers at the turn of the century to build the transcontinental railways, and hired thousands of workers every year, many of them from the Italian peninsula. These new immigrants, who did not all return to the mother *paese* when the work dried up in the winter, converged on Montréal. There they found a number of Italian institutions and could obtain services in their own language. In 1905, nearly 4,000 of these migrant workers spent the winter in the city, served by the Italian-speaking Madonna del Carmine parish, which had opened its doors that year at the corner of Amherst and Dorchester.[10]

Montréal's Little Italy, as we know it today, was born on St. Lawrence Boulevard to the north of a little railway station built in 1878 in the Mile-End district by the Canadian Pacific Railway, at Bernard Street. Drawn by the opportunity of tending their own garden plots on the vacant land there and by the lower cost of housing in Mile-End, Italian-speaking Montrealers soon converged on the northern part of the Main—so many of them, in fact, that the community opened the city's second Italian parish, Madonna della Difesa, in 1910. In 1919, a church was built on Dante Street, at the corner of Henri-Julien, near what was then called the

Bargain hunting on the Main, 1958.

THE CANADIAN PACIFIC RAILWAY STATION AT MILE END, BEFORE 1913

In 1876, a railway was built to link up Montréal with the new areas being settled in the lower Laurentians. The Quebec, Montreal, Ottawa and Occidental Railway line ran along des Carrières Street and crossed the Main via an overpass at what is now Bernard Street, before continuing on to Saint-Jérôme. A railway station was built on this site, as a way station for passengers and freight. A small Italian-speaking community sprang up around this pole, many of them maintenance of way workers, and eventually grew into Little Italy as we know it today. The photo shows the station as it appeared before it was enlarged in 1913. Metal milk cans left by farmers are waiting on the platform to be taken to market, evidence that the northern reaches of St. Lawrence Boulevard at this time were still largely rural. ◆

Marché du Nord.[11] It became the centre of the new community. By 1921, there were already nearly 14,000 Italian-born Montrealers near Jean-Talon Street.

REPOSITORY OF HISTORIC MEMORIES

While the Eastern European Jews arriving at the turn of the 20th century already had a longstanding urban tradition, many of them possessing a solid background in industrial trades and commerce, most of the Italians arriving at the same time were from rural areas, and worked as day labourers in Montréal on excavation and infrastructure projects. This initial social disparity did much to forge each community's specific cultural identity and define their courses following the Second World War, when they left the neighbourhood. The Jews, with greater social mobility, began a new migration to the western part of the city after 1950, strongly encouraged by the opening of the Sir Mortimer B. Davis Jewish General Hospital in 1934 at the corner of Côte Sainte-Catherine and Côte-des-Neiges. The great wave of post-war migration took the Italians to the farmland under residential development in the northeastern part of the island. In both cases, the Main would remain a precious symbol of the roots of their Montréal identity, recognized as a repository of their community's memories.

Chinese immigration to Canada, on a smaller scale numerically, began in the mid-19th century, as the first mines and factories were opening on the country's West Coast and looking for inexpensive labour. The construction of the transcontinental Canadian railway in about 1880 gave added impetus to this population shift, but was accompanied in British Columbia by particularly virulent anti-Chinese racism. Despite this obstacle, however, by 1901 Canada had close to 17,000 Chinese immigrants, 888 of them on the Island of Montréal. Most of these new Montrealers came to the city to escape the discrimination they encountered in Western Canada, and very often chose to make their living by opening laundries, a business where they faced little competition. Many of them set up shop between 1894 and 1911 along St. Lawrence Boulevard, around de la Gauchetière Street, where there was already a bustling and ethnically diverse business district. It was the part of the Main that Montrealers have long known as Chinatown. Nevertheless Canada's racist ethnic policies, the lack of ready capital and the hostility they encountered hindered the expansion of the Chinese community, and by 1951 it had only 1,524 members in Montréal.

THE MADONNA DELLA DIFESA CHURCH
Built in 1919, at a time when there was tremendous growth in the neighbourhood north of the Canadian Pacific tracks, the church still reflects the spirit of the first Italian-speaking immigrants to Montréal, in its architecture and its interior decoration.

Via San Lorenzo
Citta di Montreal
Quebec

CHINATOWN, THE MAIN, 1959
Reacting to Chinese immigration to the West coast of Canada starting in the mid-19th century, in 1884 the federal government began forcing all potential immigrants to pay a special head tax. Between 1881 and 1885, 15,000 Chinese came to the western provinces, where they worked laying railway tracks, in mines, sawmills and canneries, or as domestic servants. Ottawa eventually yielded to lobbying from xenophobic, racist circles and attempted to limit the number of Chinese immigrants by raising the tax to $100 in 1900, then to $500 in 1903—effectively shutting off the flow of Chinese immigrants to Canada. In 1923, a very restrictive immigration act was passed, replacing the head tax, and would remain in force until it was partially abolished in 1947. These exceptional measures had an immediate impact on Chinese communities across Canada, especially the one in Montréal, which up until the 1960s grew only very slowly. ◆

New Migrations, New Contributions

For nearly thirty years, from the beginning of the First World War in 1914 to the enf of the Second World War in 1945, fewer immigrants came to Canada's shores. The 1914-1918 conflict made travel to North America on a large scale almost impossible, while the stock market crash of 1929 had a devastating impact on the world economy and hence on international immigration. During these three decades, there was no influx of new blood into the neighbourhoods around St. Lawrence Boulevard, and the cultural communities that had taken root there flourished with no significant contribution from the outside. The period between the wars on the Main nonetheless saw some clear social and economic developments. Those immigrants who had arrived at the turn of the century became fully integrated into their new country during these key years. They learned the local languages, consolidated existing businesses or launched new ones and, above all, when they could, sent their children to pursue their studies at Montréal universities.

Most of the immigrants who had arrived early in the 20th century did so well in Montréal that with the return of peace and prosperity after 1950, they deserted Plateau Mont-Royal en masse and settled in the new middle-class suburbs around

魁北克省
蒙特利爾市
聖羅倫大道

A brass band in Little Italy, circa 1985.

the city. The neighbourhoods they left behind did not remain empty for long, however, as a new and even larger wave of immigrants soon arrived. Looking for inexpensive housing and services suited to newcomers, post-war immigrants naturally gravitated to the Main. There they found a neighbourhood that had been claimed two generations earlier by Eastern European Jews, Italians in the first wave of immigration and Chinese. So it was that Greeks, Portuguese and Hungarians, to mention only the largest of these communities, settled in Montréal in a neighbourhood that already bore the obvious traces of the ethnic communities that had come before them. The Jewish community, in particular, which was moving out as the new arrivals crowded in, left a number of synagogues and cultural buildings that would be transformed into churches or meeting places of another style altogether.

In 1970, Montréal had 45,000 inhabitants born in Greece, 20,000 from Portugal, 20,000 from Hungary, not to mention large numbers of Germans, Poles, Ukrainians, Romanians and people from the Baltic countries who had fled the aftermath of the war and the Communist advance into Eastern Europe after

Σάυτ Λόρα
Μόυτρεαλ
Κεμπὲκ

PORTUGUESE IMMIGRANTS IN HALIFAX HARBOUR, EN ROUTE TO MONTRÉAL, CIRCA 1953

The first group of Portuguese immigrants in the post-war period, some 179 people, sailed on the *Saturnia* in 1953 and arrived in Halifax and Quebec City. In the 1950s, several thousand of their compatriots, mostly from the Azores, would follow. The majority of these newcomers already had jobs when they arrived in Canada, and simply had to report to their new employers. Some went to work on farms in Quebec and Ontario, others joined maintenance of way crews on the railways in remote areas, while others were hired to work in mines and large industrial plants.

Montréal's Portuguese community was born in the late 1950s along the Main. In 1958, the first issue of *Luso-Canadiano* appeared, published by the Canadian Portuguese Association, headquartered since 1956 at the corner of the Main and Sherbrooke, in the Godin Building. The institution moved to Saint-Urbain Street, just south of Rachel, in the early 1970s, where it now occupies the former Khevra Shas synagogue. Another newspaper appeared on April 25, 1961, called *A Voz de Portugal*, and is located on the Main, between Duluth and Rachel, to this day.

The Portuguese community here also founded social and sports clubs and a Catholic Portuguese mission in 1964 under the name of Mission Santa-Cruz. It remained for a few years at 4440 Clark, in the old Neighbourhood House building, once owned by the Jewish community. In 1984, Portuguese Catholics purchased the former Mount Royal Protestant elementary school, at the corner of Rachel and Clark streets, and in early 1990 built a new church on an adjacent lot. The community also opened a senior citizens' home.

In 1964, the Portuguese democratic movement of Montréal was founded, and was initially located at 4297 St. Lawrence Blvd., near Parc du Portugal. It was followed by a credit union for Portuguese Montrealers, in 1969, whose first head office was on Pine Avenue, near the Main. Since 1980, the financial institution has been situated at 4244 Saint-Laurent Boulevard. The Portuguese referral and social promotion centre was opened in 1972, with the support of many other community organizations. Its main mission is to offer front-line services to Portuguese immigrants.

Today Montréal's Portuguese community has a number of folk-dancing troupes and social and sports clubs, most of them still located along the Main. There are about 40,000 Montrealers of Portuguese origin, and while they are increasingly moving to other parts of the city, their cultural and social life continues to be centred around the Main. In 1975, the Quebec Ordre des architectes presented the community with a collective award in recognition of its exceptional contribution to revitalizing and developing Plateau Mont-Royal. ◆

1945. Almost all of these immigrant groups created their own little communities along St. Lawrence Boulevard. During the 1980s and 1990s, other newcomers made their contribution to the Main, in particular Arab-speaking immigrants from North Africa, Spanish-speakers from South America, immigrants from Indochina, both Francophones and Anglophones from the Caribbean and Africa and others from the Indian subcontinent, adding new colours and voices to the existing mosaic. Immigration has become a very visible part of Montréal life in the past two decades, and many areas are now shining examples of the city's ethnocultural diversity—such as the Côte-des-Neiges, Parc Extension and Saint-Michel districts. Only a small fraction of newcomers now settle for good along the Main or visit it regularly. In the eyes of many Montrealers, nonetheless, Saint-Laurent Boulevard still personifies cultural diversity better than any other part of Montréal, and gives these cultures an opportunity to express themselves in all their glory.

PORTUGUESE RELIGIOUS PROCESSION, CIRCA 1985
A little St. Teresa of Jesus takes part in the Santa-Cruz festival, escorted by a few angels.

Rua São Lourenço
Cidade de Montreal
Quebeque

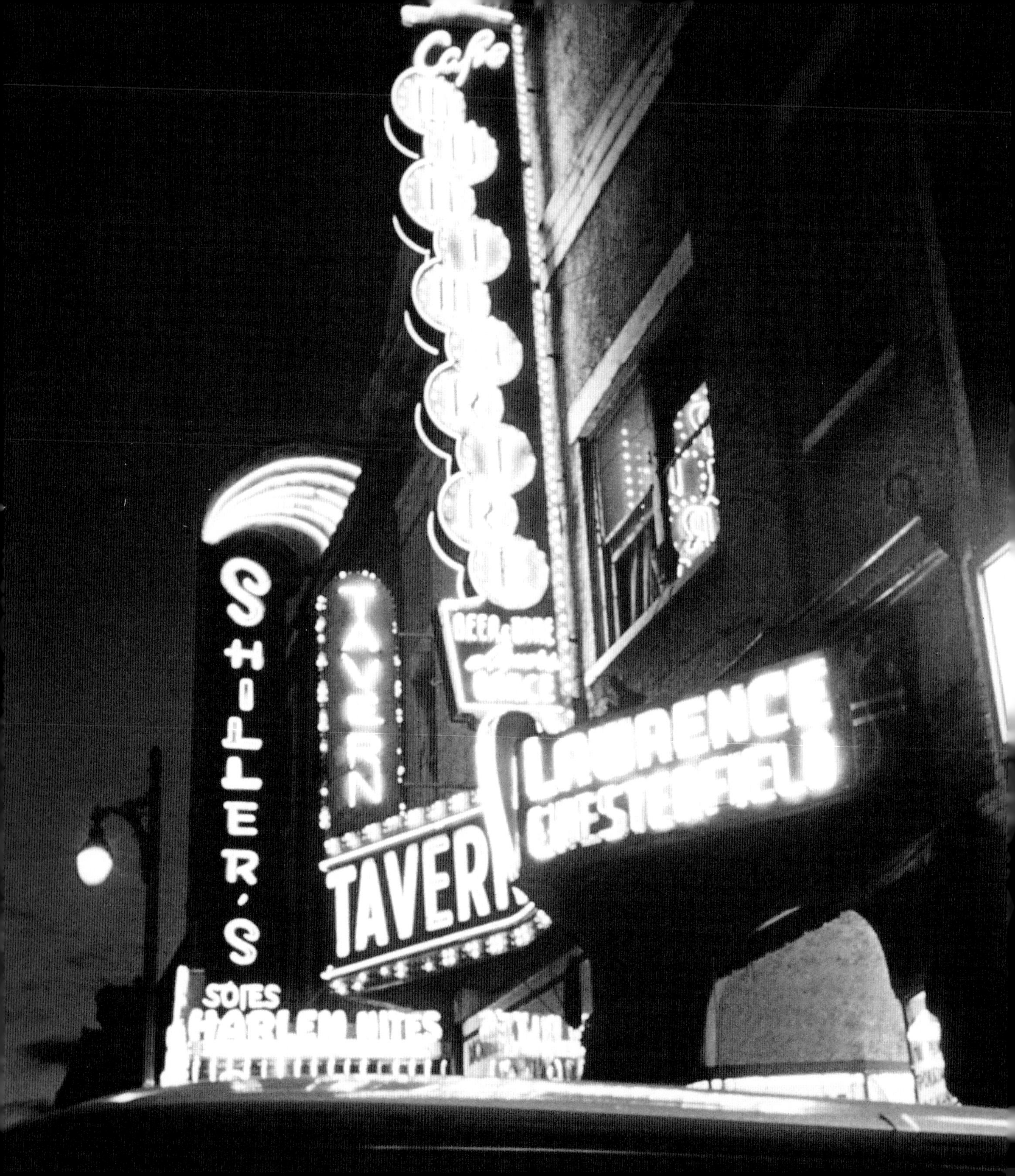
Cafe
SHILLER'S
TAVERN
TAVER
LAURENCE
HARLEM NITES

Boulevard of Cultural Innovation

SITUATED ON THE EDGE OF TWO WORLDS, THE MAIN ATTRACTED
MARGINAL CHARACTERS AND CREATIVE FRENCH- AND ENGLISH-
SPEAKING MONTREALERS. FRENCH CANADIANS, IN PARTICULAR, WERE
DRAWN TO IT TO EXPERIMENT WITH NEW FORMS OF CULTURAL EXPRES-
SION AND ESCAPE THE INFLUENCE OF THE CHURCH.

THE MONUMENT NATIONAL

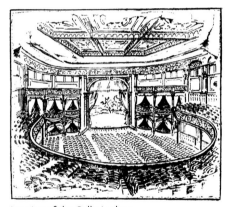

Interior of the Salle Ludger-
Duveray at the Monument
national, 1893.

Left page:
**NIGHTTIME ON THE MAIN,
CIRCA 1960**
Taken from the corner of the Main
and St. Catherine, looking north,
this photo shows the marquee of
the famous Café Montmartre and
Shiller's fabric store.

The Main was more than just the point where immigrant communities and French-
and English-Canadian society converged. Although it played this key role in Montréal
as the first forms of multi-ethnicity appeared, the Main was also the perfect testing
ground for cultural experimentation. It must be understood that at the turn of the
20th century, even more than today, the neighbourhood around the Main was a
dividing line between two very distinct worlds in Montréal: the French-speaking
Catholic east and the Golden Square Mile of the Anglo-British in the west. Between
these two groups, resembling tectonic plates pushing up against each other, the
Main was like a fissure where the prevailing social conventions and moral imperatives no longer applied. A fault line marked by constant cultural transition and
the tides of immigrants moving in and out, it was a sort of permanent social fringe
in the very heart of the city, the perfect middle ground for artistic experimentation.
"A street of perpetual renewal, where cultures and aesthetics collide and melt
together, the Main is the theatre where anything is possible, because it is not subject to the authority of a single power."[1]

For close to a century, one building in particular would symbolize the vibrant
social creativity of the Main and joyously embody the virtues of multiculturalism
before the term was ever coined: the Monument national.[2] Initially designed in
the early 1880s by the Association Saint-Jean-Baptiste[3] as a shining symbol of the

THE MONUMENT NATIONAL, CIRCA 1940

When it was completed in 1893, the Monument national towered over its surroundings. Designed by architect Joseph Venne in an eclectic Baroque Revival style, with a huge theatre seating close to 1,500, the building nevertheless ended up serving a much different public than its founders had intended. For European immigrants were pouring into Montréal after 1900, and the Main was swept by waves of newcomers arriving in the port and pushing northward. One of these communities in particular, the Jewish one, would make the Monument national the main venue for its cultural activities in the years between the wars. Yiddish theatre was a fixture there for over half a century. The Monument national would be not only a beacon for Montréal's immigrant communities, but also the cradle of French-language song and theatre in Quebec, until the battle against organized crime, along with urban renewal megaprojects in the 1960s, lowered the curtain on its years of glory. In 1971, the National Theatre School of Canada purchased the building which, like the rest of the neighbourhood, was in a sorry state. Five years later, the Monument national was classified as a historic building by the Ministère des Affaires culturelles du Québec. It took almost another twenty years before the building was completely renovated, however, in 1993.

French-Canadian presence in the heart of the English-speaking city, the Monument national had barely been inaugurated in 1893 when the project took directions unforeseen by its nationalist founders. The imposing size of the original building was intended to make it a spectacular affirmation of the Francophone presence on the Main. Among other purposes, with its 1,550-seat theatre it was to steal the thunder of other proposed sites slightly farther north on the same street. In fact, there was talk of making the Monument national the centrepiece of a French-style boulevard along the Main, but in the end the plans came to naught. Yet rather than becoming a respectable middle-class theatre district and a reflection of the political aspirations of the French-Canadian elite of the day, the neighbourhood around St. Lawrence Boulevard quickly attracted precisely those whom that slice of society rejected.

It was not only the immigrants, newly arrived in the port of Montréal, who dashed the hopes that the Association Saint-Jean-Baptiste had cherished for this great north-south corridor at the turn of the century. The city's rapidly growing population and the increasing mechanization of production processes gave birth to a large working class in the city, which in itself represented a radically new phenomenon. The industrialization of the Main and the attendant levelling of social conditions led to the rise of a truly urban mass culture for the first time in Montréal, one visible on St. Lawrence Boulevard as it was nowhere else in the city. From the beacon of good bourgeois morals that its founders had imagined, the Monument national was instead transformed by the early 20th century into a temple of popular culture and a showcase for unrestrained modernity. Women, who featured little in the plans of the patriotic society, would claim the Monument national for their own and, through the many different roles they would play on St. Lawrence Boulevard, forge a new order of relationships between the sexes.

The Birth of Burlesque and Film

By the end of the 19th century, the Main had already hosted the first variety shows to be presented in Montréal. Indeed, a whole range of productions designed to appeal to popular tastes was playing on the Boulevard, in the form of vaudeville or of theatre as such, or other huge productions. There were also places designed

LAURENT-OLIVIER DAVID (1840-1926).
A journalist, political activist and pillar of French-Canadian nationalism, Laurent-Olivier David was assigned in 1874 to organize the celebrations to mark the 40th anniversary of the Association Saint-Jean-Baptiste, an organization founded in 1834, in hopes of bringing together under its banner all the Francophones scattered throughout North America. This led to the idea of a new building that would embody the ambitions of the Association and signify its pre-eminence in the nationalist movement. The project stagnated for a number of years, until David, elected President of the Association in 1888, overcame numerous obstacles and saw it through to completion. When the Monument national was inaugurated on June 25, 1893, it symbolized the nationalist aspirations of French Canadians in Quebec's metropolis. ◆

THE CANTON OPERA, 1993
The operatic tradition at the Monument national is at least as old as the Yiddish theatre there. In 1897, an Oriental Opera Company was already playing at the famous building. The Chinese presence in the city dated from the same time as the great wave of Jewish immigrants from Eastern Europe, and the vast majority of Chinese arriving in Montréal at this time were from Canton. Little is known about the history of this art form in Montréal, though, and for long periods there is no record of it at all on the Main.

The Yuet Sing (song of Canton) company, founded in 1970, played for several years at the Monument national. The photo shows the troupe at a production put on in 1993 at the Holiday Inn Centre-ville, in the heart of Chinatown. ◆

to appeal to public curiosity, such as the Musée Éden, which opened in 1894 in the Monument national itself. These events and attractions drew a highly diverse crowd, often the whole family, looking for entertainment, excitement and sometimes even a bit of culture in the form of operettas, classical theatre and concerts. The Main was also witness to the first attempts in Montréal to establish French-language theatre; the *Soirées de Famille* ran there from 1898 to 1901, and the *Théâtre Français* opened a few years earlier.[4]

The Éden was home to a Francophone troupe as of 1894, while the Gaiety,[5] founded in 1891, served more of an Anglophone audience. But it was not only the two dominant language groups in the city who converged on the Main looking for culture. An Oriental Opera Company was formed at the Monument national in 1897, and mounted shows inspired by Chinese tradition in the all-new theatre, although its audience was essentially limited to the Cantonese community of Montréal. Throughout the 20th century, in various forms, the heirs of these first Asian artists put on works performed in the China of their forebears. Yiddish-speaking Jews, with their own theatre traditions, attended the first performance in Canada of a Yiddish play, in 1896, in that same building: *King Lear*, by Jacob Gordin. The event, organized by impresario Louis Mitnik, was such a success that for half a century the Main was the heart of Yiddish theatre in Canada. As Israël Medres explains:

Customers at the entrance to the Musée Eden, circa 1935.

MUSÉE EDEN POSTER, 1894
The Musée Eden opened in
the basement of the
Monument national in 1894,
displaying for public
enjoyment various historical
tableaux of life-size wax
figures, in mainly Canadian
scenes. It also titillated
visitors with more shocking
scenes drawn from current
events, including the
execution by guillotine in 1894
of anarchist Santo Caserio, the
man who had assassinated
French President Sadi Carnot.
Starting in 1897, the museum
also offered the public short
films made by a firm
belonging to Thomas Edison,
and variety shows in French. It
remained in operation until
1940, its continuing popularity
due above all to its collection
of wax figures. ◆

**BARNUM & BAILY CIRCUS
ON THE MAIN, 1895**
The Main had always been
linked with public entertainment
and shows, but never more so
than the day when the Barnum
& Baily Circus, "The Greatest
Show on Earth," paraded its
elephants down the middle of
the street. This photo shows the
pachyderms filing past the
St. Lawrence Market, just across
from the Monument national.
To judge by the crowd and the
young boys on the roof of the
market, circus animals were a
tremendous attraction in those
days. That Barnum & Baily came
to Montréal should not surprise
anyone who knows the history
of this U.S.-inspired circus. In
the last years of the 19th
century, this type of spectacle
was already travelling from one
city to the next by train, and
even organized a European tour
from 1897 to 1902.

" Montréal was always an important centre for Yiddish theatre. There were years when Yiddish productions were mounted every night of the week. All the stars of the American Yiddish theatre performed at the Monument National Theatre on Main Street near Dorchester. All the plays written for the Yiddish stage from dramas to comedies were presented there. Not one reputable actor or actress and not a single important Yiddish play failed to appear in Montréal.

(...) For immigrant Jews who had never seen Yiddish theatre in the old country, the Monument National was simply the paradise of the new world.[6] "

At the turn of the 20th century, great technological innovations would make possible a mass audience as well as the construction of large theatres on the Main. While electricity, sound systems, inexpensive public transit and a certain type of monumental architecture all played a role in bringing culture to the masses, none had as much impact as film. In just a few years, moving pictures shaped the popular imagination and created a dream world that reached even the most poverty-stricken and isolated members of society, bringing together individuals from very different cultural and linguistic backgrounds. The honour of ushering in the era of film went to a theatre in the Robillard Building[7] on the Main, at the time known as the Palace Theatre. The first film was shown in Montréal, based on a patent by the Lumière brothers of Paris, on June 27, 1896, marking the birth of a means of conveying ideas and forms whose impact is still felt just as powerfully over one hundred years later. Anticipating the extraordinary promise of the silver screen, a few months later, in May 1897, the Éden brought film to the Monument national.

It was another theatre in the famous building, the Starland, which opened in 1907, that would take credit for making film accessible to all Montrealers, and whose influence would spread rapidly to every district of the city. But the Starland did more than screen imported films, mainly from the United States, most of them lasting only a few minutes. Between these shows, comedians would take the stage to perform very simple burlesque routines, making the audience laugh with their witticisms and ridiculous antics. Not long after the First World War, the Starland expanded its appeal and its audiences, outdoing its many competitors on the Main by hosting the first bilingual troupes of the time, including Arthur Petrie. The French-speaking masses were delighted with this type of unpretentious entertainment and demanded more, so enthusiastically that new and little-known

AN AMATEUR JEWISH TROUPE IN FRONT OF THE MONUMENT NATIONAL, 1914
On June 21, 1914, the lyric society of the Young Men's / Young Women's Hebrew Association played the cantata *Ruth* by composer Alfred Gaul at the Monument national. On either side of the door were posters announcing the event in Yiddish and English, while above the door on the right-hand side, an Italian-language doctor advertised an "*Officio Medico Italiano*" in the building.

MENASHA SKULNIK (1892-1970)
Polish-born Skulnik emigrated to the United States in 1913 and was involved in the early days of the modernist adventure of the Yiddish Art Theater as one of its most talented players. Skulnik soon became a star in this professional troupe and appeared many times in Montréal, where Yiddish-speaking theatre goers enjoyed avant-garde theatre. Here he is seen in 1925, playing the character of the poor devil who seems to have the whole world against him. ◆

MOLLY PICON (1898-1992)
Born in New York to immigrant parents, Molly Picon appeared on the stage at a very young age. In 1919, she married playwright Jacob Kalich, who opened the doors of professional Yiddish theatre to her and launched her career in the early 1920s, in both Europe and the United States. With her tiny stature, she often played the role of an innocent boy or heart-warming clown, winning her kudos on Broadway and in Hollywood. She appeared in Montréal starting in the early 1930s, and last appeared at the Monument national in 1957, just before the Yiddish theatre moved to the city's west end. The photo shows her on stage in about 1925. ◆

PROGRAM FOR A PERFORMANCE BY MAURICE SCHWARTZ AT THE MONUMENT NATIONAL, 1955
All the great names in 20th-century American and European Yiddish theatre appeared in Montréal many times during their careers. From December 24 to 28, 1955, for example, impresarios Mitnik and Schochat presented the great Yiddish-speaking actor Maurice Schwartz (1890-1955) in a play adapted from I. J. Singer's *Brothers Ashkenazi*. A proponent of Modernism, Schwartz was the founder, in 1918, and director of the Yiddish Art Theater in New York, a troupe dedicated to performing great Jewish literary works on stage. Whenever he came to Montréal it was considered a tremendous event in the Jewish community—even in 1955, he could fill the main theatre at the Monument national four nights running. ◆

figures could dare to make a career out of it. They included Olivier Guimond Sr., Eugène Martel, Rose Ouellette (La Poune) and Juliette D'Argère. All made their mark on French-Canadian culture and paved the way for a generation of performers who would soon benefit from another great technological leap forward, television.

GROWTH OF A FRANCOPHONE ARTISTIC MILIEU

In those days, audiences on the Main enjoyed slapstick, burlesque and maudlin melodramas. But a wind of reform was sweeping the Monument national, looking to update Francophone theatre as it had been played in Montréal for a number of decades, by imposing modern forms such as those already being performed in Europe. The avant-garde movement took to the boards at the Monument national during the 1923-24 season, featuring *Soirées de Famille* (Family evenings), Vildrac, Ibsen and Jules Romains and other attractions. For the first time, the French-Canadian elite could enjoy top-flight theatre and get a taste of the experimental theatre put on by the most daring artistic movements. This period also saw the emergence of modern trends in Yiddish theatre, as the Vilnius and Habimah troupes visited Montréal from Eastern Europe, both of them advocating realism and restraint in acting. These two worlds, Jews and French Canadians in Montréal, now found they had something in common on the Main, not entirely by chance.

> "[Trans] Members of the Yiddish community certainly attended French-language theatre, even amateur productions. There is also no doubt that French Canadians were familiar with the modern experiments taking place in Europe at the turn of the century, either because they had seen them first-hand when travelling in Europe or because they had read about them. But there is every reason to believe that the leaders of the renewal in French-language theatre in Montréal also saw Jacob Adler and his disciples, who shared their stage.[8] "

The contribution of the Main to local culture extended beyond theatre and comedy. Quebec song would literally be born there, before spreading around the globe. In 1921, folk musician Conrad Gauthier founded the *Veillées du bon vieux temps* at the Monument national, an old-time celebration that would be held year in, year out, up until the mid-1940s. These shows echoed a past that recently

The avant-garde movement took to the boards at the Monument national during the 1923-24 season, featuring *Soirées de Famille* (Family evenings), Vildrac, Ibsen and Jules Romains and other attractions. For the first time, the French-Canadian elite could enjoy top-flight theatre and get a taste of the experimental theatre put on by the most daring artistic movements.

OLIVIER GUIMOND SR., STAR OF THE MONUMENT NATIONAL
The Arthur Pétrie burlesque troupe began playing at the Starland in 1919, and soon began featuring a comedian as yet unknown to the Quebec public, known as Tizoune. The character was an overnight sensation, and Olivier Guimond Sr. very quickly became a star, with his comic routines drawing on American slapstick, but delivered in both languages. His son, Olivier Jr., also launched his career on the Main in his father's troupe, and later took burlesque to new heights on television.

MADAME BOLDUC (1894-1941)
Born Mary-Rose-Anne Travers, in Newport, on the Gaspé peninsula, she moved to Montréal in the early 20th century after marrying Édouard Bolduc, and became Quebec's best-known popular singer during the period between the wars. She started her career at the Monument national in 1930.

urbanized rural French Canadians still held dear, but they were more than a tribute to people's attachment to the land. They also served as a springboard for a wide variety of talented performers who would play to packed houses for almost 20 years, including Hector Pellerin, Hector Charland, Eva Alarie, Jeannette Teasdale and Ovila Légaré.

One of Gauthier's protégés, Mme Bolduc, would soon draw on the novelty of sound recordings to create the first large Francophone audience and propel Quebec song to previously unequalled heights. Born Mary Travers in a village in the far-off Gaspé, for decades Mme Bolduc embodied the hopes and emotions of an entire people through her highly colourful performances of her own compositions. Her celebrity drew her away from the Main, though, and in the late 1930s she set off on a tour of French-Canadian communities throughout North America. Others followed in her wake, including Alys Roby, who would be a hit ten years later at the Monument national, and who launched a movement that led straight to the explosive focus on identity and art that appeared in the wake of the Quiet Revolution.

A Decisive Contribution by Feminists

While talented women, through popular song and theatre, laid the foundations of Quebec culture as we conceive of it today, other no less daring women were paving the way for the legal emancipation of their sisters and forging new roles in society for them. In 1898, the "ladies" of the Association Saint-Jean-Baptiste, also housed in the Monument national, drew up a first feminist action plan based on hygiene and health, education and the need for changes in legislation affecting women. These were, naturally, the wives and daughters of the exclusively male membership of the association. They were part of the great reform movement among the Francophone middle class and took part from the very beginning, albeit in the shadows, in efforts to promote the interests of French Canada. Among them were such prominent figures as Marie Gérin-Lajoie, Justine Lacoste-Beaubien, Caroline Béïque, Idola Saint-Jean and Joséphine Dandurand. A first official meeting of the group of patronesses of the Association Saint-Jean-Baptiste was held on the Main in 1902, confirming their influence and launching a movement that would win women the vote in federal elections, in 1917, and later recognition of their status as legal persons.

MARIE GÉRIN-LAJOIE (1867-1945)
Up to the turn of the 20th century, Francophone women wishing to better their lot had to join organizations motivated mainly by Anglophone concerns, like the Montreal Local Council of Women, founded in 1893. This situation changed radically when Caroline Béique and Marie Gérin-Lajoie launched the Fédération nationale Saint-Jean-Baptiste, in 1907, with the goal of winning for women the right to higher education, equality in the eyes of the law and the vote. The Fédération, closely linked to the Association Saint-Jean-Baptiste, organized its social struggles from offices located in the Monument national, on the Main, up until 1925. For close to 25 years, Marie Gérin-Lajoie presided over the organization, an umbrella group for various feminist groups working in the fields of philanthropy and education. ◆

In 1904, this same group founded an institution known as the *École ménagère*. It would play a key role in women's advancement, giving them access to the world of higher education, which up until that time had been all but inaccessible. This inspired the opening of Collège Marguerite-Bourgeois, in 1908, run by the sisters of the Congrégation Notre-Dame, which turned out the first women graduates in Quebec. They also took an interest in working conditions for women in shops and factories, leading to the rise of the first female Francophone trade associations in that same decade. Up until 1925, when the Fédération nationale Saint-Jean-Baptiste left the Main and moved north to Sherbrooke Street, the Monument national was the birthplace of feminist currents of thought whose repercussions can still be felt in Quebec society today.

As the modern era dawned in Montréal, it was not only well-dressed women and rising stars who frequented the Main. Other women were there, too, although the anonymity of the big city has concealed their exact identities. Yet we know that they also played a central role in this far-reaching redefinition of the relations between the sexes. Some were trade unionists, others young seamstresses, night-club waitresses, strip-tease artists and prostitutes. In fact, at the end of the Second World War, from 2,000 to 3,000 women were practising the world's oldest profession in the 300 brothels that lined St. Lawrence Boulevard between Sherbrooke and Craig streets.[9] The illicit appeal of Montréal's great artery was founded on a certain "liberated" concept of femininity. Despite its sometimes sordid side, the explicit sex trade on the Lower Main, the greater freedom in women's roles and the rejection of rigid Victorian morals heralded changes that within a few decades would sweep through Quebec society as a whole:

> " The Lower Main represented a challenge to the middle class separation of women and the public world of commerce and industry. In this case, it was the commodification of women's sexuality to create physical intimacy in public that reinforced the border status of the *Main*.[10] "

Although this might seem a rather odd context for promoting women's rights, it was nevertheless on the Main that many women were able to earn meagre wages for the first time, freeing them from thankless household tasks. In a way, the Lower Main sounded the death knell, in the early 20th century, of that social order that confined women to the home, far from the great economic and political movements that marked the Montréal of the time. More visible socially, able to travel to and from work on their own and even to demand their rights by banding together in exclusively female trade unions, women factory workers paved the way for wholesale changes in the way women were seen in Montréal society. Although it is true that women were exploited in the factories and behind the doors of certain houses of ill-repute, the Main nonetheless thoroughly undermined the perception of women that had prevailed in Victorian society.

In a way, the Lower Main sounded the death knell, in the early 20th century, of that social order that confined women to the home, far from the great economic and political movements that marked the Montréal of the time.

Gangsters, Striptease Artists and Stars of the Stage

Other equally impressive talents sprang up on the Main, although they certainly did not draw their inspiration from Quebec rural life and the humble condition of women factory workers. In keeping with the complex blend of high culture and popular appeal that had characterized the Monument national since its beginnings, a Canadian operetta society founded by Honoré Vaillancourt appeared on the stage of the famous theatre in 1921. Later, in 1936, the same building was the scene of a program hosted by Charles Goulet, known as the *Variétés lyriques*. Both these artistic movements would work hard, despite limited resources, to promote a French-language professional theatre in post-war Montréal. In fact, it often played just a stone's throw from the Main. The winner in this race, however, was Gratien Gélinas, who assembled a Quebec theatrical review with his *Fridolinades* cycle,

STRIPTEASE ARTIST LILI ST. CYR, CIRCA 1946

One of the best-known striptease artists on the Lower Main, Lili St. Cyr, was born Maria Van Shaak in 1918, in Minneapolis, Minnesota. Her career began in California, in San Francisco to be exact, when a nightclub hired her first of all as a dancer and later to disrobe in front of an audience. Elegant, racy and with great stage presence, Lili St. Cyr met with phenomenal success in her own country and toured the major U.S. centres. In 1944 she came to Montréal, where she played until 1951, an indication of the city's stellar reputation in those times. She often resorted to subterfuges as she removed her clothing bit by bit—in this case a fake parrot!—to avoid breaking municipal morality codes. ◆

STRIPTEASE ARTIST LILI ST. CYR, CIRCA 1946

Poster from *Fridolinons* 41, 1941.

GRATIEN GÉLINAS IN THE ROLE OF FRIDOLIN, 1945
Thanks to Gratien Gélinas, the Quebec review rose from the ashes as a
theatre genre, combining burlesque antics with pointed social commentary
on French Quebec at the time. The *Fridolinades* series, launched in 1938 and
starring the mischievous Fridolin, met with enormous popular success and
played at the Monument national until 1946.

running from 1938 to 1946, in the theatre managed by the Association Saint-Jean-Baptiste. Following the good-natured Fridolin, Gélinas created a new character in 1948, again at the Monument national: Tit-Coq, who incarnated in this painful post-war period the quest for excellence by a Francophone society battered by world events.

While a wind of artistic creativity blew along the Main in the post-war years and sowed its seeds throughout Quebec, ominous developments were also brewing there. Over time they would end up shouldering aside the once-flourishing theatres and artistic venues. A whole series of major social and technological changes, including talking movies, radio and television, hit the Main south of Sherbrooke especially hard. Each scientific advance brought with it new means of communication, luring once-faithful patrons away from the Main and carrying the voices, images and ambitions of the stars born there to far-off audiences. No longer did one have to go to the theatre itself to hear and see the stars of the day, when in households all over Quebec one could hear the songs of Mme Bolduc or watch the comic antics of Olivier Guimond, better known back then as "Tizoune junior."

Gradually abandoned, the theatres where families and fashionable couples had once flocked were now converted into nightclubs, cabarets, jazz joints and strip-tease bars. What the nascent and still prudish medium of television could not offer because of its dubious morality was displayed for all to see on the Main, with Lili St. Cyr and other striptease artists.

Last Gasps on the Lower Main

For a number of years, in the late 1940s and early 1950s, the Main was home to clubs that for Francophone Montrealers were something quite new, including the Faisant Doré, a delight for lovers of French song. In those days, Edith Piaf was performing at the Monument national with the Compagnons de la chanson, and Charles Trenet, Jean Clément and Henri Salvador also appeared there. In 1950, the Théâtre du Rire founded by Henri Poitras brought Rita Bibeau, Jean Duceppe, Olivette Thibault and Juliette Béliveau to the stage of the Monument national, while in 1956 the Théâtre du Rideau Vert made its home for a few months in the well-loved fixture. But these were the last gasps, for then the Lower Main sunk into marginality for good, while its built heritage fell into disrepair.

THE *CANADIAN AMBASSADORS*, CLUB MONTMARTRE, 1937

The artists and staff of the Club Montmartre posing for posterity on October 6, 1937. The musicians, from left to right: Willy Wade (drums), Harold "Steep" Wade (alto saxophone), Myron Sutton (alto saxophone, band leader), Benny Montgomery (trumpet), Bill Kersey (tenor saxophone), Brad Moxley (piano). On Willy Wade's left: Adophe Allard, owner of the Montmartre, in front of Myron Sutton: Willie Légaré (manager of the Montmartre).

The *Canadian Ambassadors* was a well-known Canadian band that played in Montréal from 1932 to 1941. The Club Montmartre was located at the corner of Ste. Catherine Street. It was a favourite hangout of jazz fans in the 1930s, and black musicians often played there. ◆

A FLYER FROM CONNIE'S INN, CIRCA 1932

Connie's Inn, which opened in the early 1930s at the corner of Ste. Catherine, was one of the city's foremost jazz clubs in those years, and perfectly reflected the atmosphere on the Main at the height of Prohibition in the United States. The club lured passers-by with a combination of the Folies Bergères, American jazz and sexual promiscuity— a specialty of the neighbourhood. ◆

DANCERS AT THE CAFÉ SAINT-MICHEL, CIRCA 1949
Tina Brereton, Bernice Jordan and Marie-Claire Germaine were part of the first all-Canadian black chorus line.◆

A Descent into Hell

By definition a transitional space between larger groups with relatively fixed territorial and linguistic boundaries, the Main had always harboured more than its share of crime and questionable behaviour in the eyes of upright citizens. A wide-open district permanently linked to the port, throughout the 20th century it was home not only to the strangeness of new immigrants but also to the disreputable places where Montrealers came to escape the grip of dominant social forces. This fragile coexistence that held the unusual, the unknown and the unacceptable in a delicate balance began coming apart when narrow-minded authorities in the United States imposed a total ban on the sale, manufacture and consumption of alcohol in 1920. Until Prohibition in the U.S. was repealed in 1933, it diverted to Montréal a number of notorious criminals and many delinquent citizens who could no longer quench their thirst south of the border. During this time, most of the clubs, bars and theatres south of Sherbrooke street fell into the hands of organized crime, a phenomenon that picked up speed during the Depression years and then the war, to the point that it even sank the flagship of the Boulevard,

ILLEGAL LOTTERY ON THE MAIN, CIRCA 1935
A common scene on the Main in the 1930s: a group of gamblers crowded round a table, placing illegal bets, in the middle of the street. The photo also shows the main entrance to the Monument national across the street, and posters for the films showing that week.

THE MAIN AND ONTARIO IN 1952
At the corner of Ontario, an electric tram prepares to negotiate the slope up
to Sherbrooke. Immediately behind it can be seen the Molson Bank, today
the Native Friendship Centre of Montreal.

the Monument national itself. Following the Second World War, the famous theatre lost its occupants one by one and gradually languished. A descent into hell began, which Michel Tremblay described in his play *Sainte-Carmen de la Main*, in the words of one of the characters, "Silver-Dollar-Maurice":

"Poor Carmen! You don't know them! You take old 'Silver-Dollar-Maurice's' word for it: people who end up on the Main don't want to be saved. I've been working the Main for twenty-five years, night and day, month after month, year after year. The Main is my mother! She brought me up. She gave me my first rap on the knuckles, my first kick in the ass and my first dose. There isn't a square inch of the Main that I don't know by heart. And believe me, kiddo, it's not you who's gonna change her. She's seen lots before you, and tougher too, and she knew how to handle them."[11]*"*

UNDER THE WRECKER'S BALL

By the early 1950s, the situation had deteriorated to such a point that municipal authorities were powerless. Two ambitious young lawyers, Jean Drapeau and Pax Plante, took part in a public investigation into crime, in 1954, and spoke out against the blatant prostitution in the neighbourhood, the illegal betting, shady bars and lax policing.

When Drapeau was elected Mayor in October of that same year, he promised to tackle the problem — and was true to his word. He did everything possible to stamp out vice and corruption, even demolishing whole residential blocks around the Main. In no time at all, the southern section between Saint-Antoine and Ontario streets was razed, replaced by parking and vacant lots. The construction of the Habitations Jeanne-Mance, Place des Arts, the Saint-Laurent metro station, the Palais des Congrès and the Guy Favreau Complex divided up and rent the oldest urban fabric surrounding the artery, while the widening of Dorchester Boulevard and the digging of the Ville-Marie Expressway finally robbed it of any meaning or relevance to the city. The Lower Main, the promised land for generations of immigrants, whose reputation extended throughout the country and even beyond its borders, trembled beneath the jackhammers of demolition crews and served for a time as a laboratory for urban renewal trends.

Two ambitious young lawyers, Jean Drapeau and Pax Plante, took part in a public investigation into crime, in 1954, and spoke out against the blatant prostitution in the neighbourhood, the illegal betting, shady bars and lax policing.

CHAPTER 4

Boulevard of the Technological Revolutiom

AFTER WATCHING ITS INDUSTRIES TAKE FLIGHT IN THE 1950S, SAINT-
LAURENT BOULEVARD HAS BEGUN THE SLOW, GRADUAL CLIMB BACK UP.
NOW SOME OF THE MOST AVANT-GARDE CULTURAL MILIEUX IN THE CITY
ARE FOUND ON THE MAIN. CHIEF AMONG THEM IS MULTIMEDIA,
WHICH IS COMPLETELY TRANSFORMING THE URBAN LANDSCAPE.

A DIFFERENT KIND OF IMMIGRANT COMES TO THE MAIN

While the Lower Main suffered the slings and arrows of urban planners in the
1950s and 1960s, at the same time the section of the Boulevard between
Sherbrooke and Bernard was losing its industries at a rapid pace. The garment
industry, which had brought prosperity to the artery in the first half of the 20th
century, suddenly fled, leaving behind immense industrial spaces built to hold
workshops for hundreds of workers. Most garment manufacturers simply closed
or migrated northward along the Boulevard up to Chabanel Street, where they
formed a large block of factories.[1] In the post-war period, some well-established
and now more prosperous cultural communities left the district; the Jews headed
west, while the Italians moved farther east, into Ville Saint-Léonard. These turn-
of-the-century immigrants were replaced by more-recent newcomers from Greece,
Portugal and, later, from Asia, Africa and the Caribbean. For a time, the successive
waves of departures exhausted the Main, leaving the district to totter into urban
marginality and dilapidation. The photographs taken at this time by Sam Tata and
Edward Hillel, for instance, speak volumes.

During this desperate period, the Main appeared like a no-man's land, where
those who had trouble identifying with dominant sexual practices and ideas con-
gregated, along with others looking to explore new forms of social relations.
Suddenly abandoned, the Main became a space where the usual norms were

Left page:
3536 SAINT-LAURENT BOULEVARD
Ex-Centris, the film and new
media complex, is the new
"beacon" on the Main. Since
1999 it has been offering film
buffs an exceptional variety of
high-quality programs. The
Centre comprises three high-tech
theatres and is recognized as a
world-class centre for image
research.

The same intersection, looking south, with the Woolworth Building on the right and the marquee of the Café Canasta farther down. Behind it can be seen the huge Hydro-Québec building, inaugurated in 1962, clearly showing the impact on the Main of major urban renewal projects in the 1960s.

pushed aside, making room for experimental behaviours unacceptable elsewhere. People on the fringes of society, indifferent to their run-down surroundings and unwelcome in other neighbourhoods: "Prostitutes (both male and female), transvestites, 'b-girls', butch lesbians and gay men."[2] St. Lawrence Boulevard took in new migrants, from around the city this time, giving rise to the first neighbourhood that sexual minorities could truly call their own. So it was that in the mid-1970s the Lower Main saw the rise of clubs celebrating transvestites. L'Androgyne, a bookstore specializing in gay and lesbian literature, opened in 1973, just north of Prince-Arthur Street. It soon became a social and political centre for the gay community, hosting exhibitions, lectures, readings and debates on the theme of new sexual orientations. L'Androgyne moved from its cramped quarters to Amherst Street in 2001, in the heart of Montréal's "new" gay village.

An Unexpected Venue for Quebec Literature

Almost at the same time as so many different people were seeking their identities in so many different ways on the Main, great writers were surfacing in Montréal, many of them from this neighbourhood. They would celebrate the diffuse, inexpressibly poetic character of the area. With them, the Main made its entry into Quebec and Canadian and even international literature, as an unexpected venue for cultural encounters and the blending of identities. An awareness emerged that the old street that had served as the backbone of the metropolis for so many decades was once again being transformed, this time into a place that lent itself to creation, social marginality and new currents of thought. The chaotic, disorderly face of the Main, which had both delighted and surprised those who had ventured there in the early 20th century, survived the flight of its former economic functions and shone brilliantly in the works of a new generation of artists. Jean-Jules Richard in *Carré Saint-Louis*, Yves Thériault in *Aaron* and A.M. Klein in *The Second Scroll* described a Main marked by discreet exoticism, a mixture of cultural division and urban decay. Hugh MacLennan, author of *Two Solitudes*, came to Montréal in 1935. Toward the end of his life he wrote this about the Main:

The tentative and gradual renewal in the 1970s and 1980s, based on a flurry of modest ventures, would pave the way, in the 1990s, for an artistic outpouring of a kind rarely seen on the Main. The complete restoration of the central theatre of the Monument national, dating from 1893, and a few years later of the Théâtre du Nouveau-Monde, just west of it on Sainte-Catherine, breathed new life into the Lower Main.

" The Main astonished me, and it still does. I had walked the streets of many famous cities in England, Europe and the United States, but this was something new. Most of the stores had Jewish names. It was probably the most creative Jewish area in North America, more so even than New York, and out of it emerged men who became distinguished lawyers, businessmen (some on the grand scale), poets, novelists and musicians. In future years I was to discover that some of my dearest and most admired friends had grown up in this district. The Main has been the most astonishing forcing house in Canada for culture and business. ... the Main continues in its old role as a prime seed-bed of a growing nation.[3] "

POSTER FOR THE FILM *IL ÉTAIT UNE FOIS DANS L'EST*, 1973
Il était une fois dans l'Est, by director André Brassard, brought characters from such Michel Tremblay plays as *Les belles-sœurs*, *Hosanna* and *La Duchesse de Langeais* to the screen. Among others, it featured Denise Filiatrault (on the poster), Michelle Rossignol, Frédérique Collin, Sophie Clément and André Montmorency, in a *danse macabre* ranging from the Main to the straight-laced parish halls of Plateau Mont-Royal.

MORDECAI RICHLER AND MICHEL TREMBLAY

Such descriptions of the Main and the surrounding neighbourhood first appeared in the post-war period, challenging long-standing perceptions and throwing new light on a unique part of Montréal. The warmth of the immigrants who called St. Lawrence Boulevard home, sometimes despite miserable living conditions and economic exploitation, overflowed the neighbourhood and extended to larger and larger segments of the population. The district drew people's attention because of its unusual cultural practices, the sense that one was sheltered from the dictates of social convention and, above all, because of the frequently contradictory influences that coexisted there. Through novels, poetry and song, in a tremendous variety of languages, the Main gained an international audience, becoming what was probably Canada's most famous street. People flocked there from all over the country, some as tourists looking to be surprised and shocked, others because the goods and sensations offered on and around the Main could sometimes be had for the price of a mouthful of bread.

Two writers in particular revealed a special affection for the Main in their works, and would carry the reputation of St. Lawrence Boulevard and its surrounding streets far beyond Quebec's metropolis. Mordecai Richler and Michel Tremblay, each from a very particular cultural perspective, would offer up stirring images of Plateau Mont-Royal to a vast readership, engendering an important literary renewal in the early 1960s in both English Canada and French Quebec. The unforgettable characters created by the two novelists, often emotionally crippled or living in a demimonde on the fringes of society, would introduce people far removed from the Main to life there in the post-war years. Richler's cynical and cheeky tone and Tremblay's very intimate descriptions also greatly contributed to creating a vision of the Main in the collective imagination, one that grew to become a universal myth. Who does not know Germaine Lauzon or Rose Ouimet, from *Les Belles-Sœurs*, or Duddy Kravitz and his French-Canadian girlfriend, Yvette Durelle, from the novel of the same name? Once again, the street became an unusual and fertile meeting ground between innovative artistic movements and a social milieu with no fixed boundaries.

Some of the descriptions left by Richler accurately describe the general decay of the neighbourhood, but at the same time convey its inhabitants' sense of living in an environment where bursts of vital energy were possible:

"To a middle-class stranger, it's true, one street would have seemed as squalid as the next. On each corner a cigar store, a grocery and a fruit man. Outside staircases everywhere. Winding ones, wooden ones, rusty and risky ones. Here a prized plot of grass splendidly barbered, there a spitefully weedy patch. And endless repetition of precious peeling balconies and waste lots making the occasional gap here and there. But, as the boys knew, each street between St. Dominique and Park Avenue represented subtle differences in income. No two cold-water flats were alike. Here was the house where the fabulous Jerry Dingleman was born. A few doors away lived Duddy Ash, who ran for alderman each election on a one-plank platform: provincial speed cops were anti-Semites. No two stores were the same, either. Best Fruit gypped on the scales, but Smiley's didn't give credit.[4]"

These lines give a clear impression of the way better-off Montréal neighbourhoods scorned the Main, particularly the newly arrived Jews there, and of the conviction shared by its residents that in time they would succeed. One finds much the same view in Tremblay's plays or autobiographical novels, in which another minority, equally disdained, gradually began to think of itself as a nation. The two communities quite naturally converged on this common ground, and learned to coexist as they patiently adjusted to Montréal's cultural diversity:

"Mercedez avait rencontré Béatrice dans le tramway 52 qui partait du petit terminus au coin de Mont-Royal et Fullum pour descendre jusqu'à Atwater et Sainte-Catherine, en passant par la rue Saint-Laurent. C'était la plus longue ride en ville et les ménagères du Plateau Mont-Royal en profitaient largement. Elles partaient en groupe, le vendredi ou le samedi, bruyantes, rieuses, défonçant des sacs de bonbons à une cenne ou mâchant d'énormes chiques de gomme rose. Tant que le tramway longeait la rue Mont-Royal, elles étaient chez elles, elles faisaient tous les temps (...). Mais quand le tramway tournait dans la rue Saint-Laurent vers le sud, elles se calmaient d'un coup et se renfonçaient dans leurs bancs de paille tressée: toutes, sans exception, elles devaient de l'argent aux Juifs de la rue Saint-Laurent, surtout aux marchands de meubles et de vêtements (...)[5]."

WHERE CREATORS MEET

The run-down neighbourhood would be home to another emblematic literary figure, an Anglophone this time: Leonard Cohen, born in the very well-off city of Westmount, but a child of the Main by choice. Since 1972, the universally recognized poet and singer has spent part of each year in a house just off Saint-Laurent Boulevard, where he has written some of his most famous songs. His incongruous presence, in the shadow of the now-silent factories, is a sort of manifesto for the counter-cultural values he represents, and has been remarked on in the French press as well:

> [Trans] Leonard Cohen, one of the multiple characters in his book *Death of a Lady's Man*, is standing in his kitchen on Vallières Street, just across from Parc du Portugal, a guitar in his hands and a new song on his lips. (...) In the poet's study are a modest, nearly monastic wooden table, children's photographs, a few books on mythology, and two manuscripts, one of them with the very apt title of *My Life in Art*.
> 'I am in favour of the Free State of Montréal,' he says. 'To be absolutely clear, I do not live in a country, I live in a neighbourhood, a completely separate universe, entirely removed from modern civilization, the normal world of business, money, success and social climbing. I don't have any appetite for all that, I never have had. I'm happy just to do what I have to do, and let life take care of the rest.'[6]

Cohen, writer of the famous song *Suzanne*, has an unobstructed view down Saint-Laurent Boulevard to the port, from whence he regularly escapes to his property on the island of Hydra, in Greece, or to Los Angeles. As he steps through his door en route for other lands, a woman guides him: "Now Suzanne takes your hand / and she leads you to the river / she is wearing rags and feathers / from Salvation Army counters/ and the sun pours down like honey / on our lady of the harbour."[7]

The popularity of the Main in French and English literature in Canada was just one aspect of its slow recovery, the signs of which were increasingly visible north of Sherbrooke Street after the mid-1960s. It was as if the loss of its former industrial and commercial roles had finally freed up new creative energy, which could be born and grow only atop the ruins of a submerged empire. The huge spaces

Claire Savoie, 1986. In the 1970s and 1980s, many avant-garde artists found a place for themselves in the old Vineberg Building, dating from 1912, at the corner of Duluth. It became a co-operative of studios, known as 4060 Saint-Laurent.

Sculptor Pierre Granche at 4060 Saint-Laurent Boulevard, 1986.

Painter Jacques de Tonnancourt at 4060 Saint-Laurent Boulevard, 1986.

Jean Faucher in his studio at 4060 Saint-Laurent Boulevard, 1986.

THE CINÉMA PARALLÈLE IN 1992
The Cinéma Parallèle, opened in 1971 by Claude Chamberland at 3682 St. Lawrence, in the Baxter Block, brought experimental screenings and film research to Montréal, along with video, theatre and art. It moved to the Ex-Centris complex in 1999, where it continues to present independent programming in the heart of the ultra-modern building at 3530 Saint-Laurent Boulevard. ◆

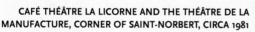

CAFÉ THÉÂTRE LA LICORNE AND THE THÉÂTRE DE LA MANUFACTURE, CORNER OF SAINT-NORBERT, CIRCA 1981
Many small theatres presenting experimental theatre and other creative works sprang up along the Main in the 1960s, playing Quebec plays and foreign works in translation. ◆

formerly occupied by nimble-fingered women workers would now serve as lofts and artists' studios, and the first were home to some of the champions of modernism in Quebec, artists like Louis Archambault, Jacques de Tonnancour, Albert Dumouchel, Joan Esar, Roland Giguère, Betty Goodwin and Gérard Tremblay.[8] The magnificent buildings that had previously been written off were taken over by institutions or groups at the cutting edge of creation in Quebec— including the exceptional Monument national, which the National Theatre School of Canada purchased in 1971 and renovated completely in the mid-1990s.

A Central Role in the History of Cinema

In 1963, Paul Buissonneau founded the Théâtre de Quat'Sous in a former synagogue just steps away from the Main, and named it in tribute to the masterpiece of a playwright and champion of the lower classes, Bertolt Brecht. Slightly farther south, at the corner of Milton and Clark, in the former Shaare Tfile synagogue, the Cinéma Élysée appeared in 1959. For decades it was one of Montréal's major theatres, reconfirming the central role played by Saint-Laurent Boulevard in the history of cinema in Montréal. The innovative character of the Main could again be seen in 1971, when Claude Chamberland founded the Cinéma Parallèle just north of Prince-Arthur. Although it was a small theatre in terms of seating, it nevertheless played a very large part in the development of different artistic media, including film research, theatre and plastic arts.

In fact, it is the Cinéma Parallèle that has been hosting the Festival international du nouveau cinéma et des nouveaux médias de Montréal for close to thirty years now. Ten years later, in 1981, the Théâtre de la Manufacture opened in turn on the Main, just south of Sherbrooke, with the La Licorne café-theatre, which would become a venue for daring experimentation by a whole new generation of creators. The days of major projects were still to come, however. Nearly twenty years would go by before Saint-Laurent Boulevard attracted big-name cultural institutions. As Bourassa and Larrue point out,[9] no one was interested in competing with Sainte-Catherine or Saint-Denis. The Main remained true to itself and preferred the risk of small theatres and avant-garde creations to proven values, choosing danger over comfort. It was part of its nature, and a sign of good health.

The magnificent buildings that had previously been written off were taken over by institutions or groups at the cutting edge of creation in Quebec—including the exceptional Monument national, which the National Theatre School of Canada purchased in 1971 and renovated completely in the mid- 1990s.

From Factories to Art Studios

The Regroupement des travailleurs et travailleuses du sexe, also known as Stella, which works to defend the interests of sex workers.

The huge abandoned industrial buildings on Saint-Laurent Boulevard were also ideally suited to forms of art calling for lots of room, including dance. During the 1980s and 1990s, the Main attracted a number of avant-garde troupes, specifically to the Balfour building on the corner of Prince-Arthur and the Cooper building, just north of Bagg Street. La La La Human Steps, the Margie Gillis Dance Foundation and the Compagnie Marie Chouinard set up in this district that not so long before had danced to the tune of sewing machines and strikers' shouts in the streets below. The Vineberg building, north of Duluth Street,[10] built at the dawn of the 20th century by the manufacturer of the same name, is today a particularly relevant example of recycling. 4060 Saint-Laurent Boulevard was divided up and sold to photography agencies, architectural firms, artists and gallery owners, some of them famous for a time, including Articule, Dare-Dare and Dazibao. One of the occupants, Peter Gnass, when asked by a French journalist in 1994 whether there wasn't a danger of the Main being yuppified, replied: "It's important that it not become too upmarket. But I don't think that's a danger for Saint-Laurent Boulevard. Since I've been here, I've seen lots happen, businesses open and close. In the end all that doesn't change much. It's still the same disorder."[11]

The tentative and gradual renewal in the 1970s and 1980s, based on a flurry of modest ventures, would pave the way, in the 1990s, for an artistic outpouring of a kind rarely seen on the Main. The complete restoration of the central theatre of the Monument national, dating from 1893, and a few years later of the Théâtre du Nouveau-Monde, just west of it on Sainte-Catherine, breathed new life into the Lower Main. Farther north, new initiatives, including the arrival of the Just for Laughs Museum and the Académie nationale de l'humour in the old Ekers brewery in 1993, brought new life to a particularly run-down stretch. Other newcomers added their own special flavours to this area, including the Montréal Native Friendship Centre, in the old Molson bank at the corner of Ontario. Faithful to its historical vocation, the Main also welcomed the place of worship of a new religious minority in Montréal, with an Afghan mosque. And this same section of the Main has been home since 1999 to the Regroupement des travailleurs et travailleuses du sexe, also known as Stella, which works to defend the interests of sex workers.

North of Sherbrooke, the transformation has been even more spectacular, with a whole new theatre complex appearing in June 1999 on a vacant lot just south

MARGIE GILLIS IN FULL FLIGHT
The artist performing her own choreographic work, entitled *Torn Roots, Broken Branches*.

of Prince-Arthur. Ex-Centris, founded by Daniel Langlois, bills itself as a cinematographic research laboratory. The complex has three theatres boasting cutting-edge technology and devoted to independent films, including the Cinéma Parallèle theatre, which manages its own programming. The institution is also intended as a gathering place where artists, filmmakers and producers can forge and maintain close ties with their counterparts in new media. Nearby, restaurants, bars and

FESTIVAL INTERNATIONAL NUITS D'AFRIQUE DE MONTRÉAL
A group of musicians performing on the festival stage. The
festival has been held on Saint-Laurent Boulevard since 1987.

stores showcase the daring of Montréal architectural design, so much so that the
Main has now become a centrepiece of trends in this form of artistic expression
in Montréal. Just south of Saint-Joseph Boulevard, Espace Go inaugurated, in
1995, a multipurpose space for contemporary French-language theatre, thereby
restoring the Main to its place at the heart of avant-garde artistic creation.

A Multimedia Explosion

With its fragmented, original and eclectic face, the Main would also attract many cultural events, which found it an appropriate stage for daring of every kind. The Montréal Fringe Festival has been playing there since 1991, featuring all aspects of the performing arts, from theatre to dance, music and puppet shows. Another is the Festival international des Nuits d'Afrique de Montréal, which has played annually at the Le Balattou dance hall since 1987. Saint-Laurent Boulevard owes its current surge in energy to a new technological revolution, though—one that oddly echoes the days when electricity was introduced in manufacturing. In 1986, Daniel Langlois founded Softimage, a firm specializing in 3D film animation software. The company opened on the Main, just north of Sherbrooke, in the old Reitman's clothing factory, which dated from the previous technological revolution. The astounding success enjoyed by Softimage (bought out by Microsoft, the American multinational, in 1994) has brought about a new era in the growth of Saint-Laurent Boulevard, one in which existing buildings and architectural resources are being completely recycled, with respect for their historical and cultural character.

Multimedia companies, proliferating in Montréal since the early 1980s, quickly found that Saint-Laurent Boulevard was a great place to start up and grow. In December 2000, the 159 computer and multimedia firms on the Main, mostly between Sherbrooke and Van Horne Avenue, represented 20% of such businesses in central Montréal and the largest concentration of computer and multimedia firms in Quebec. In fact, the energy in this leading-edge economic sector closely resembles the "upside-down T" shape of the garment and fur manufacturing industry in the early days of the Main. Multimedia firms today stretch along an east-west axis from Atwater to Papineau, including Old Montréal, and from north to south, along the traditional axis of Saint-Laurent Boulevard. Essentially, what we are seeing is a re-creation, with entirely different working conditions, of the facilities and social milieux that inspired Montréal's first great industrial expansion.

This geographic coincidence, a century apart, of the manufacturing and multimedia revolutions in Montréal is taking place without many new buildings going up—ample confirmation that the great axes of historical development, like the Main, continue to play a very important role in the city. Old urban forms living on in this way can be explained largely by the fact that the designers and workers

Saint-Laurent Boulevard owes its current surge in energy to a new technological revolution, though—one that oddly echoes the days when electricity was introduced in manufacturing, and whose impact is only just beginning to be felt along the Boulevard.

Still from the film *Jurassic Park*, directed by Steven Spielberg, Softimage. Still from the film *Men in Black*, directed by Barry Sonnenfeld, Softimage.

in these new industries are seeking a dense and compact urban context, something unconventional, highly adaptable, in the centre of the city and suited to often explosive growth. The typical buildings from the old manufacturing days are ideally suited to these requirements, first of all because they have long been deserted and hence are not very expensive. The old clothing factories are also easy to reconfigure, high-ceilinged, very safe, and easy to convert into open areas. They are also part of a quality urban environment, where one can find inexpensive housing and excellent services, including a variety of restaurants, grocers, boutiques and other stores. The marginal historical impact of the automobile in the development of Montréal's central neighbourhoods makes it quite feasible to do without a car for one's professional life, another strong argument in favour of these old urban structures.

This transformation is easily visible in the section of the Main extending from Sherbrooke to Mont-Royal Avenue, where graphic design, digital imaging, film production and distribution, Internet, video production, recording services and computer consulting firms now account for about 30% of the workforce. This adds up to nearly 1,500 workers generating annual sales of close to $800 million. On this same part of the Boulevard, nearly one-quarter of the available rental space is occupied by businesses of this kind, followed by restaurants, cafés and bars, representing 27% of workers and 16.5% of floor space, respectively. Then come professional offices, food stores and property administration, in that order. In comparison, manufacturing firms, formerly so omnipresent on this part of the Main, now represent only 1% of occupied rental space. There is every reason to believe that the in-depth transformation that started several years ago around Prince-Arthur Street will soon extend north and south to take in other buildings now deserted or unused.

Rebirth of the Faubourg Saint-Laurent

The far-reaching metamorphosis of the Main continues unabated, while new renovation projects take shape on the construction site or the drafting board. In late 2001, a major real-estate developer announced plans to change the face of the block between Sainte-Catherine, René-Lévesque, Clark and the Main, to make it a showcase of culture and artistic creation in Montréal. The idea in this case would be to preserve the historic late-19th-century facades of all the buildings involved, while gutting the interiors. Shops would be located on the ground floor of this new "Cité des arts," while the upper floors would be co-owned by cultural organizations in the worlds of visual arts, dance and theatre. This new urban development, in the heart of the former red-light district, would spell a complete makeover for this part of the Main, known in the days of the French regime as the Faubourg Saint-Laurent.

It would restore some glory to an area that was so popular in the early 20th century, when the Monument national, now renovated, was shining bright and when the Main gave birth to the first Francophone mass culture in Quebec. This stretch of the Main also includes such venerable institutions as the Café Cléopâtre and the Montreal Pool Room, true relics of that period. The relocation of the Club Soda nightclub and the construction by the Société Saint-Jean-Baptiste de Montréal of a student residence on the corner of René-Lévesque Boulevard should also help to revitalize this area, which has been particularly neglected over the past 20 or 30 years. The upcoming expansion of the Al-Ummah Al-Islamiah mosque, located near the Monument national on Saint-Dominique Street, should bring even more diversity to the area.

The far-reaching metamorphosis of the Main continues unabated, while new renovation projects take shape on the construction site or the drafting board.

A Symbol of "Montreality"

Despite its cyclical setbacks and the assaults it has suffered over the years, Saint-Laurent Boulevard continues to rise from its ashes, to the point where it is now considered a symbol of what Montréal is all about. After all, very early on it embodied many changes that marked the history of the city: urban settlement outside the walls, industrialization, multiculturalism, the rise of artistic currents and, more recently, the advent of new technologies. Protected by this dividing line between two major language groups, a whole series of daring movements and new social realities emerged on the shores of the Main before setting sail for more distant horizons. In the 20th century, especially, it became — sometimes against its will — a place of transgression, welcoming and celebrating all that was marginal, exceptional and un-assimilatable. Here, at different times, immigrants, feminists, avant-garde artists, gangsters, radical anarchists and sexual minorities coexisted, mostly taking little notice of each other. This linear and constantly evolving space has been a melting pot for disparate, eclectic and antagonistic elements reflecting the modern age, with eventual and unexpected repercussions for the city all around it.

For the history of the Main is the history of how all Quebec, and even Canada, was plunged into a new form of society dominated by the meeting of opposites, a sharp collision of identities and ideas. That which is truly modern in Montréal first appeared on this unusual boulevard that crosses the heart of the city like an incandescent fault line through once-indistinguishable territories. It was the Main, nearly a century ago, that first experienced multiculturalism in Quebec and welcomed great waves of immigrants. In fact, the cultural aspects of the Quiet Revolution were largely launched here on the Main. Events that were at the time highly innovative appeared on Saint-Laurent Boulevard in an unpredictable and seemingly unrelated series of forms and manifestations. In this skilfully orchestrated disorder were also a number of technological revolutions related to film, industrial architecture, the use of electricity in manufacturing and, finally, multimedia.

BERSON L. & SON FUNERAL MONUMENTS, CIRCA 1985
Founded in 1922 by Louis Berson, at a time when the Main was the undisputed centre of Jewish life in Montréal, the company has barely changed in 80 years and still offers its services to a community that has essentially migrated to the city's west end. The gravestones, easily visible from the street, remind passers-by of a time when the Hebrew alphabet was a common sight on the Main.

The Main has always anticipated the shape of things to come in Montréal, and it continues to do so today, as the artery is under assault by new forces that are sure, in the long term, to transform the interiors of the urban structures and buildings inherited from another age.

The Main has always anticipated the shape of things to come in Montréal, and it continues to do so today, even as the artery is assaulted by new forces that are sure, in the long term, to transform the interiors of the urban structures and buildings inherited from another age. The Main is becoming a place where Montrealers' love of life finds a remarkable outlet, in particular at events like the *Frénésie de la Main*, when the stretch between Sherbrooke and Mont-Royal is closed for three days. The multitude of different ethnic groups, the variety of businesses, the quality of the services available and the architectural diversity are among the exceptional drawing cards of the Main today. The living and ever-changing history of Saint-Laurent Boulevard, which at one time was in serious danger of disappearing, is a vitally important heritage for Montréal. For the artery represents better than any other the historic complexity of the city, the far-reaching transformations it has undergone since the very beginning and the way its inhabitants have adapted.

A Constantly Evolving Space

It is this exceptional contribution that the Historic Sites and Monuments Board of Canada recognized in 1998 when it classified the Main, from the St. Lawrence River up to Jean-Talon Street, as a historic district of national interest. The Quebec government recently granted similar recognition to certain buildings, including the Monument national, the Grothé building at the corner of Ontario and the Godin building at the corner of Sherbrooke. Saint-Laurent Boulevard, anchored to the river of the same name, shows us just how Montréal's unique essence emerged and developed, in all its complexity and its particular social and cultural forms. Still a vibrant and constantly changing place, the Main defies all trends and lives on, fuelled by the energy of its residents. There is no need, in the circumstances, to stimulate the creativity or originality of this great artery or to preserve its intensity. Instead, the Main simply expects us to protect its physical integrity and that special fusion of roles responsible for its charms and attractions, and to resist on its behalf the powerful forces of uniformity and commercialization at work around the globe.

NOTES

PROLOGUE

Birth of a Great Urban Artery

1. Louise Dechêne, "La croissance de Montréal au XVIIIᵉ siècle." *Revue d'histoire de l'Amérique française*, Vol. 27, No. 2, September 1973, p. 163-179.
2. Alan Stewart, "Settlement, Commerce and the Local Economy," in *Opening the Gates of Eighteenth-Century Montréal*, Phyllis Lambert and Alan Stewart, Ed. Montréal: Canadian Centre for Architecture, 1992, p. 54.
3. Phyllis Lambert, "Removing the Fortifications: Toward a New Urban Form," in *Opening the Gates of Eighteenth-Century Montréal*, Phyllis Lambert and Alan Stewart, Ed. Montréal: Canadian Centre for Architecture, 1992, p. 79.
4. Jean-Claude Robert, *Atlas historique de Montréal*. Montréal: Art global et Libre expression, 1994, p. 73.
5. Jean-Claude Robert, "Réseau routier et développement urbain dans l'Île de Montréal au XIXᵉ siècle," p. 99-115, in Horacio Capel and Paul-André Linteau, Ed., *Barcelona-Montréal: développement urbain comparé*. Barcelona: Publications de la Universitat de Barcelona, 1998, 498 p.

CHAPTER 1

Boulevard of the Industrial Revolution

1. From Jean-Claude Robert, *Montréal, 1821-1871. Aspects de l'urbanisation*. PhD thesis in History, École des hautes études en sciences sociales/Université de Paris I, 1977.
2. The building was demolished in about 1960. The site is now the Parc des Amériques.
3. The area is called Mile-End because at the time there was a clearing between what is now the Hôtel-Dieu hospital and Mont-Royal, which was later used as a racetrack and military parade ground. At the turn of the 19th century, there was about one mile between the north side of this land and the city limits, where Bagg Street now runs.
4. *Historical Atlas of Canada*, Vol. III. Toronto: University of Toronto Press, 1990, plates 13, 19.

5. Jean-Claude Robert, *Atlas historique de Montréal*. Montréal: Art global / Libre expression, 1994, p. 85.
6. Mercedes Steedman, *Angels in the Workplace. Women and the Construction of Gender Relations in the Canadian Clothing Industry, 1890–1940*. Toronto: Oxford University Press, 1997.
7. *Historical Atlas of Canada*, Vol. III. Toronto: University of Toronto Press, 1990, plate 14.
8. Mercedes Steedman, p. 42.
9. Hirsch Hershman: "25 yor yidish arbeter bavegung in Montreal," in *Unzer Vort*, Montréal, March 2, 1928, p. 5. The complete text was published in *Bulletin du Regroupement des chercheurs en histoire des travailleurs du Québec*, Spring 2000, No. 71, Vol. 26, No. 1, p. 42-60.
10. "La parade socialiste," in *La Presse*, Montréal, May 2, 1906, p. 5.
11. *Historical Atlas of Canada*, Volume III. Toronto: University of Toronto Press, 1990, plate 19.

CHAPTER 2

Boulevard of New Arrivals

1. U.S. Census Bureau, *Profile of the Foreign-Born Populations in the United States: 1997*, Special Studies P23-195, August 1999, p. 9.
2. Valerie Knowles, *Forging Our Legacy: Canadian Citizenship and Immigration, 1900-1977*. Ottawa: Department of Public Works and Government Services Canada, 2000, Chapter 2.
3. This building was located on the west side of Saint-Laurent Boulevard, between Guilbault Street and des Pins Avenue.
4. From the Massicotte Street albums collection, Bibliothèque nationale du Québec, Montréal.
5. Louis Rosenberg, *Canada's Jews. A Social and Economic Study of the Jews in Canada*. Montréal: Canadian Jewish Congress, 1939, table 108, p. 160.
6. Israël Medres, "Di yidishe arbeter bavegung in Kanade," *Yubl Bukh, Der Keneder Odler*, July 8, 1932, p. 79-80; to appear in French translation in winter 2002, in the *Bulletin du Regroupement des chercheurs-chercheuses en histoire des travailleurs et travailleuses*.

7. Israël Medres, *Montreal of Yesterday* (*Montreal fun Nekhtn*). Montréal: Véhicule Press, 2000, p. 214.
8. Mordecai Richler, *The Street*. Toronto: McClelland and Stewart Limited, 1969, p. 53.
9. Jacob Isaac Segal, "Late Autumn in Montreal."
10. Now René-Lévesque Boulevard.
11. Now Jean Talon Market.

CHAPTER 3
Boulevard of Cultural Innovation

1. Translated excerpt from André-G. Bourassa and Jean-Marc Larrue, *Les Nuits de la Main*. Montréal: VLB éditeur, 1993, p. 184.
2. The building is located at 1182 Saint-Laurent Boulevard, just north of René-Lévesque Boulevard.
3. Today the Société Saint-Jean-Baptiste de Montréal.
4. On Sainte-Catherine Street, where the Métropolis discotheque now stands.
5. At first located in the Robillard Building, at 972 Saint-Laurent, and later in what is now the home of the Théâtre du Nouveau Monde, at 539 Sainte-Catherine West.
6. Israël Medres, *Montreal of Yesterday. Jewish Life in Montreal 1900-1920*. Montréal: Véhicule Press, 2001, p. 92, 95.
7. Although it is in poor condition, the building still stands at 972 Saint-Laurent Boulevard.
8. Jean-Marc Larrue, *Le Monument inattendu. Le Monument national 1893-1993*. Montréal: Hurtubise HMH, Cahiers du Québec No. 106, 1993, p. 199-200.
9. Today Saint-Antoine Street.
10. Julie Podmore, *St. Lawrence Boulevard As Third City: Place, Gender and Difference Along Montreal's "Main."* Montréal: McGill University, PhD thesis in Geography, 1999, p. 205.

11. Michel Tremblay, "Sainte-Carmen de la Main." Translated by John Van Burek. Vancouver: Talon Books, 1981, p. 52.

CHAPTER 4
Boulevard of the Technological Revolution

1. The garment industry was still Quebec's sixth largest industry in 1996, with 47,141 employees working for 1,113 companies, most of them located in Montréal.
2. Julie Podmore, *St. Lawrence Blvd. As Third City: Place, Gender and Difference along Montreal's "Main."* Montréal: McGill University, PhD thesis in Geography, 1999, p. 214.
3. Preface, in Edward Hillel, *The Main. Portrait of a Neighbourhood*. Toronto: Key Porter Books, 1987.
4. Mordecai Richler, *The Apprenticeship of Duddy Kravitz*. Toronto: McClelland and Stewart Limited, 1969, p. 15-16.
5. Michel Tremblay, *The Fat Woman Next Door Is Pregnant."* Translated by Sheila Fischman. Vancouver: Talonbooks, 1981, p. 18.
6. Nathalie Petrowski, "Leonard Cohen: portrait robot d'un poète perdu," in *Le Devoir*, November 4, 1978, p. 21.
7. Leonard Cohen, *Stranger Music. Selected Poems and Songs*. Toronto: McClelland and Stewart, 1993, p. 93-94.
8. André-G. Bourassa and Jean-Marc Larrue, *Les nuits de la «Main». Cent ans de spectacles sur le Saint-Laurent Boulevard (1891-1991)*. Montréal: VLB éditeur, Études québécoises collection, 1993, p. 160.
9. André-G. Bourassa and Jean-Marc Larrue, p. 168.
10. Also known as the "4060" (Saint-Laurent Boulevard).
11. Sylviane Tramier, "Boulevard Saint-Laurent," in *Le Monde*, Paris, January 15, 1994.

BIBLIOGRAPHY

Historical Atlas of Canada. Toronto: University of Toronto Press, Vol. III, 1990, plates 13, 14 and 30.

L'avenue du Mont-Royal, un siècle et demi au cœur du Plateau. Montréal: Archives nationales du Québec, 1992, 33 p.

"Le plateau Mont-Royal." *Continuité*, No. 66, Fall 1995, p. 9-52.

Le plateau Mont-Royal au 19ᵉ siècle. Montréal: Comité logement Saint-Louis, 1984, 22 p.

ALPALHÂO, Joao Antonio and Victor Manuel PEREIRA DA ROSA. *Les Portugais du Québec: éléments d'analyse socio-culturelle.* Ottawa: Éditions de l'Université d'Ottawa, 1979, 317 p.

ANCTIL, Pierre. *Le rendez-vous manqué. Les Juifs de Montréal face au Québec de l'entre-deux-guerres.* Quebec City: Institut québécois de recherche sur la culture, 1988, 366 p.

ANCTIL, Pierre. *Tur Malka, Flâneries sur les cimes de l'histoire juive montréalaise.* Sillery: Éditions du Septentrion, 1997, 199 p.

ANCTIL, Pierre. "Le boulevard Saint-Laurent, lieu des possibles." *Continuité*, No. 88, Spring 2001, p. 24-27.

BEAUREGARD, Ludger. "Géographie historique des côtes de l'Île de Montréal." *Cahiers de géographie du Québec*, Vol. 28, Nos. 73-74, April-September 1984, p. 47-62.

BELKIN, Simon. *Le mouvement ouvrier juif au Canada, 1904-1920.* Translated from Yiddish to French by Pierre ANCTIL. Sillery: Les Éditions du Septentrion, 1999, 390 p.

BOUCHARD, Isabelle and Gabriel MALO. "Sur les traces du patrimoine juif de Montréal : les synagogues du 20ᵉ siècle dans le quartier du Plateau Mont-Royal." *Patrimoine*, Fondation Héritage Canada, Fall 2000, p. 27-29.

BOURASSA, André-G., and Jean-Marc LARRUE. *Les Nuits de la «Main». Cent ans de spectacles sur le boulevard Saint-Laurent (1891-1991).* Montréal: VLB éditeur, collection Études québécoises, 1993, 361 p.

BUMBARU, Dino. "Le grand méridien de Montréal." *Continuité*, No. 88, Spring 2001, p. 52-56.

CAPLAN, Usher. *Like One That Dreamed, a Portrait of A. M. Klein.* Toronto: McGraw-Hill Ryerson, 1982, 224 p.

DECHÊNE, Louise. "La croissance de Montréal au XVIIIᵉ siècle." *Revue d'histoire de l'Amérique française*, Vol. 27, No. 2, September 1973, p. 163-179.

DUMAS, Evelyn. *Dans le sommeil de nos os. Quelques grèves au Québec de 1934 à 1944.* Montréal: Éditions Leméac, collection Recherches sur l'homme, 1971, 170 p.

GAGNON, Gemma. *La syndicalisation des femmes dans l'industrie montréalaise du vêtement, 1936-1937.* Montréal: Université du Québec à Montréal, Master's thesis in history, 1990, 256 p.

GERMAIN, Annick. "Les quartiers multiethniques montréalais, lieux de sociabilité publique," p. 471-482, in Horacio CAPEL and Paul-André LINTEAU, Ed., *Barcelona-Montréal : développement urbain comparé.* Barcelona: Publications de la Universitat de Barcelona, 1998, 498 p.

GRAHAM, Conrad. *Mont-Royal, Ville-Marie, Early Plans and Views of Montreal.* Montréal: McGill-Queens' University Press, 1992, 159 p.

GUBBAY, Aline. *A Street Called the Main. The Story of Montreal's Boulevard Saint-Laurent.* Montréal: Meridian Press, 1989, 134 p.

HALL, Roger, Gordon DODDS and Stanley TRIGGS. *The World of William Notman. The Nineteenth Century Through a Master Lens.* Toronto: McClelland & Stewart Inc., 1993, 226 p.

HELLY, Denise. *Les Chinois de Montréal, 1877-1951.* Quebec City: Institut québécois de recherche sur la culture, 1987, 315 p.

HILLEL, Edward. *The Main, Portrait of a Neighbourhood.* Toronto: Key Porter Books, 1987, 184 p.

D'IBERVILLE-MOREAU, Luc. *Lost Montreal.* Toronto: Oxford University Press, 1975, 183 p.

KNOWLES, Valerie. *Forging Our Legacy: Canadian Citizenship and Immigration, 1900-1977.* Ottawa: Department of Public Works and Government Services Canada, 2000, 103 p.

LAMBERT, Phyllis and Alan STEWART, Ed. *Opening the Gates of Eighteenth-Century Montréal.* Montréal: Canadian Centre for Architecture, 1992, 93 p.

LARRUE, Jean-Marc. *Le Monument inattendu. Le Monument-national 1893-1993.* Montréal: Éditions Hurtubise HMH, Cahiers du Québec No. 106, collection histoire, 1993, 322 p.

LAVIGNE, Gilles. *Les Ethniques et la ville: l'aventure urbaine des immigrants portugais à Montréal.* Longueuil: Le Préambule, 1987, 215 p.

LESSARD, Michel. *Montréal métropole du Canada. Images oubliées de la vie quotidienne 1852-1910.* Montréal: Les Éditions de l'Homme, 1992, 303 p.

LÉVESQUE, André. *Virage à gauche interdit. Les communistes, les socialistes et leurs ennemis au Québec, 1929-1939.* Montréal: Boréal, 1984, 186 p.

LÉVESQUE, André. *La norme et les déviantes. Des femmes au Québec pendant l'entre-deux-guerres.* Montréal: Éditions du Remue-Ménage, 1989, 232 p.

LINTEAU, Paul-André. *Histoire de Montréal depuis la Confédération.* Montréal: Boréal, 1992, 613 p.

MARSAN, Jean-Claude. *Montreal in Evolution. Historical Analysis of the Development of Montreal's Architecture and Urban Environment.* Montréal: McGill-Queen's University Press, 1990, 456 p.

MEDRES, Israël. *Montreal of Yesterday: Jewish Life in Montreal, 1900-1920.* Translated from Yiddish by Vivian FELSEN. Montréal: Véhicle Press, 2000, 214 p.

MEDRES, Israël. *Le Montréal juif entre les deux guerres.* Translated from Yiddish by Pierre ANCTIL. Sillery: Les Éditions du Septentrion 2001, 242 p.

NADEL, Ira B. *Leonard Cohen, Le Canadien errant.* Montréal: Boréal, 1997, 382 p.

PODMORE, Julie. *Loft Conversions in a Local Context: The Case of Inner City Montreal.* Montréal: McGill University, Master's thesis in geography, 1994.

PODMORE, Julie. *St. Lawrence Blvd. as Third City: Place, Gender and Difference Along Montreal's "Main."* Montréal: McGill University, PhD thesis in geography, 1999.

RAMIREZ, Bruno. *Les premiers Italiens de Montréal. L'Origine de la Petite Italie du Québec.* Montréal: Boréal-Express, 1984, 136 p.

RAMIREZ, Bruno and Michele DEL BALSO. "The Italians of Montreal: From Sojourning to Settlement, 1900-1921." In Robert F. HARNEY and J. Vincenza SCARPACI, Ed., *Little Italies in North America.* Toronto: The Multicultural History Society of Ontario, 1981, p. 63-84.

ROBERT, Jean-Claude. "Aperçu sur les structures socio-professionnelles des villages de la région nord de Montréal, durant la première moitié du XIXᵉ siècle." In *Cahiers de géographie du Québec,* Vol. 28, Nos. 73-74, April-September 1984, p. 63-67.

ROBERT, Jean-Claude. *Atlas historique de Montréal.* Montréal: Art global and Libre expression, 1994, 168 p.

ROBERT, Jean-Claude. "Réseau routier et développement urbain dans l'Île de Montréal au XIXᵉ siècle," p. 99-115, in Horacio CAPEL and Paul-André LINTEAU, Ed., *Barcelona-Montréal : développement urbain comparé.* Barcelona: Publications de la Universitat de Barcelona, 1998, 498 p.

ROME, David. *Through the Eyes of the Eagle. The Early Montreal Yiddish Press 1907-1916.* Translations from Yiddish edited by Pierre ANCTIL. Montréal: Véhicule Press, 2001, 204 p.

ROSENBERG, Louis. *Canada's Jews.* Montréal: Canadian Jewish Congress, 1939, 418 p.

STEEDMAN, Mercedes. *Angels of the Workplace. Women and the Construction of Gender Relations in the Canadian Clothing Industry, 1890-1940.* Toronto: Oxford University Press, 1997, 333 p.

STEWART, Alan M. *Settling an 18th Century Faubourg: Property and Family in the Saint-Laurent Suburb, 1735-1801.* Montréal: McGill University, PhD thesis in history, 1988.

TASCHEREAU, Sylvie. "Nouveau regard sur les relations judéo-québécoises: le commerce comme terrain d'échanges," p. 33-49, in Pierre ANCTIL, Ira ROBINSON and Gérard BOUCHARD, Ed., *Juifs et Canadiens français dans la société québécoise.* Sillery: Les Éditions du Septentrion, 2000, 197 p.

TEIXEIRA Carlos and Victor Manuel PEREIRA DA ROSA. *The Portuguese in Canada: from the Sea to the City.* Toronto: University of Toronto Press, 2000, 238 p.

VIDAL, Laurent and Émilie d'ORGEIX, Ed. *Les villes françaises du Nouveau Monde. Des premiers fondateurs aux ingénieurs du roi (XVIᵉ–XVIIIᵉ siècles).* Paris: Somogy éditions d'art, 1999.

WEINTRAUB, William. *City Unique, Montreal Days and Nights in the 1940s and '50s.* Toronto: McClelland & Stewart Inc., 1996, 332 p.

WEISBORD, Merrily. *The Strangest Dream. Canadian Communists, the Spy Trials, and the Cold War.* Toronto: Lester & Orpen Dennys Ltd., 1983, 255 p.

WOLOFSKY, Hirsch. *Mayn Lebns Rayze, Un demi-siècle de vie yiddish à Montréal.* Translated from Yiddish by Pierre ANCTIL. Sillery: Les Éditions du Septentrion, 2000, 391 p.

PHOTO CREDITS

P. 11: *Map of the Island of Montréal and environs* (detail), after Jacques-Nicolas Bellin, 1764. Collection Centre canadien d'architecture/Canadian Centre for Architecture. **P. 14**: *Plan of the wall around the town of Montréal and the outline of its fortifications*, Louis Franquet, 1752. Ministère de la Défense, Service historique de l'Armée de Terre, France, Folio 210e. **P. 17**: *Plan of Ville-Marie and the first streets planned for the "upper town,"* François Dollier de Casson, 1672. Archives nationales de France, centre historique, K/1232, No. 43. **P. 18-19**: *A View of the City of Montreal*, James Peachey, 1784. National Archives of Canada, C-002002. **P. 22**: *Plan of the town and suburbs of Montréal*, Paul Jourdain dit Labrosse, 1767. Molson family. **P. 23**: *Montreal from Mount Royal*, Thomas Davies, late 18th century. National Gallery of Canada, Ottawa, No. 6286. **P. 24**: Plan of the proposed construction work along Saint-Laurent Street to improve *surface drainage*, September 3, 1801, Louis Charland. Ville de Montréal. **P. 25**: Boulevard de l'Opéra, late 19th century. Sketch by Georges Delfosse. From *La Presse*, May 27, 1899. Side view of the Church of Our Lady of Pity, Congregation de Notre-Dame, Montreal, QC, ca 1885, after a stereogram by Olivier. B. Buell. Notman Photographic Archives, McCord Museum of Canadian History, Montréal, MP 0000.2925. **P. 26**: Map of the City and Suburbs of Montreal, John Adams, 1825. Department of Rare Books and Special Collections Divison, McGill University Libraries. **P. 27**: Baxter Block, west side of St.Lawrence Street, Montreal, QC, ca 1918. Notman Photographic Archives, McCord Museum of Canadian History, Montréal, MP 1978.207.36. **P. 28**: Female employees of the Biltmore Shirt Co. Ltd. at work in the Balfour Building, in the mid-1930s. Private collection, Rubenstein Bros. Co. Inc. **P. 30**: *View near Mile End*, Montreal, QC, 1831, by James Duncan. McCord Museum of Canadian History, Montréal, M686. The west side of St. Lawrence Street in 1884, north of Viger. E.-Z. Massicotte Fonds, Bibliothèque nationale du Québec, 7-447. Protestant and Catholic churches in Montreal near the Molson house, July 1840. Painting by Philip John Bainbridge (1817-1881). National Archives of Canada, No. C-011877. **P. 31**: St. Lawrence Street in the early days of photography. Ville de Montréal. Gestion de documents et archives, D-112. **P. 33**: The Shamrock Lacrosse Club, 1896. E. Z. Massicotte Fonds, Bibliothèque nationale du Québec, B-174b. **P. 34**: Saint-Enfant-Jésus du Mile End Church. Undated photo, E. Z. Massicotte Fonds, Bibliothèque nationale du Québec, 7.51a. **P. 35**: Saint-Jean-Baptiste market, circa 1930. Undated photo, Ville de Montréal. Gestion de documents et archives, Z-157. **P. 36**: Town hall of the municipality of Saint-Louis du Mile-End. Undated photo, E. Z. Massicotte Fonds, Bibliothèque nationale du Québec, 7.46d. The Peck factory, ca 1915. From *Montreal Old and New*, Lorenzo Prince. Montréal: International Press, 1915, p. 313. Bibliothèque nationale du Québec. **P: 37**: Laying tramway tracks at the corner of Craig and St. Lawrence streets, 1893. Archives of the Société de transport de Montréal. **P. 38**: Corner Craig Street and St. Lawrence Main Street, Montreal, QC, ca 1910. Notman Photographic Archives, McCord Museum of Canadian History, Montréal, MP-0000.816.3. **P. 39**: The Montreal shoe trade.-No.1, Messrs Fogarty's Factory, corner Ste.Catherine and St. Lawrence main streets, Montreal, QC, 1871, by Eugene Haberer. McCord Museum of Canadian History, Montréal, M985.230.5033. **P. 41**: The Biltmore Shirt Co. Ltd. laundry, 3575 St. Lawrence, ca 1930. Private collection, Rubenstein Bros. Co. Inc. **P. 43**: A picket line, circa 1960. Photo by Michel Régnier in Montréal, Paris d'Amérique. Montréal: Éditions du Jour, 1961, p. 58. **P. 44**: A demonstration during a strike by garment workers, 1937. Archives of the International Ladies' Garment Workers' Union. **P. 45**: Cooper Building in 1952. Archives of the Société de transport de Montréal. **P. 46**: St. Lawrence Main and St. Catherine Street, Montreal, QC, ca 1905. Notman Photographic Archives, McCord Museum of Canadian History, Montréal, MP-1978.207.22. **P. 48**: Immigrants arriving at Montreal, QC, ca 1910. Notman Photographic Archives, McCord Museum of Canadian History,

Montréal, MP 1980.84.23. **P. 49**: The Beth Yehuda synagogue, circa 1908. E. Z. Massicotte Fonds, Bibliothèque nationale du Québec, 2-238-a. **P. 50**: The Ekers' Brewery. St. Lawrence Boulevard, Montreal, QC, ca 1910, by Neurdein. Notman Photographic Archives, McCord Museum of Canadian History, Montréal, MP-0000.816.5. **P. 51**: Souvenir of a bar mitzvah. Three generations of Jewish men, circa 1900. Canadian Jewish Congress National Archives, Montreal, P92/07//2. **P. 52**: Hirsch Wolofsky, circa 1926. From A. D. Hart, The Jew in Canada. Toronto: Jewish Publications, 1926. Canadian Jewish Congress National Archives, Montreal. **P. 53**: The Shaare Tfile synagogue, Austrian-Hungarian Synagogue, Milton Avenue, Montreal, QC, between 1901 and 1910. Notman Photographic Archives, McCord Museum of Canadian History, Montréal, View 10761. In front of the Warshaw store, circa 1950. City of Montréal. Gestion de documents et archives, Z-2230-3. **P. 54**: The presses of the Keneder Odler, circa 1932 .25th anniversary souvenir album, Der Keneder Odler, Montréal, 1932. Canadian Jewish Congress National Archives, Montreal. **P. 55**: Yiddish on the Main, 1958. Photograph by Sam Tata. **P. 56**: Joseph Schubert (1889-1952). Ville de Montréal. Gestion de documents et archives, Z-945-1. Schubert Baths in 1932. Ville de Montréal. Gestion de documents et archives, Z-77-1. **P. 57**: Bargain hunting on the Main, 1958. Photograph by Sam Tata. **P. 58**: The Canadian Pacific railway station at Mile End, before 1913. Canadian Pacific Railway Archives, image A-12741. **P. 59**: The Madonna della Difesa Church. Photograph by Gaby Matossian. **P. 60**: Chinatown, the Main, 1959. Photograph by Sam Tata. **P. 61**: Italian marching band, circa 1985. Photo by Edward Hillel. **P. 62**: Portuguese immigrants in Halifax harbour, en route to Montréal, circa 1953. National Archives of Canada, PA189616. Southam Inc./ The Gazette. **P. 63**: Portuguese religious procession, circa 1985. Photo by Edward Hillel. **P. 64**: Nighttime on the Main, circa 1960. Ville de Montréal. Gestion des documents et archives, A31-4. **P. 65**: Interior of the Salle Ludger-Duveray at the Monument national, 1893. From La Presse, June 24, 1893. **P. 66**: The Monument national, circa 1940. Canadian Pacific Railway Archives, image NS 3305. **P. 67**: Laurent-Olivier David (1840-1926). Undated photo, Archives nationales du Québec, "Société Saint-Jean-Baptiste de Montréal" Fonds, P 82, 1976-00-006\1. **P. 68**: The Canton Opera, 1993. Private collection

of Catherine Fung. **P. 69**: Customers at the entrance to the Musée Eden, circa 1935. "Conrad Poirier" Fonds, Archives nationales du Québec, P48, S1, P5204. Musée Eden poster, 1894. From La Minerve, August 17, 1894. **P. 70**: Barnum & Baily Circus on the Main, 1895. From the Monde illustré, Montréal, August 3, 1895, p. 194. Bibliothèque nationale du Québec. **P. 71**: An amateur Jewish troupe in front of the Monument national, 1914. From the Canadian *Jewish Chronicle*, June 1914, Canadian Jewish Congress National Archives, Montreal. Menasha Skulnik (1892-1970). YIVO Institute, New York, papers of Jacob Mestel, 280 (474.74). Molly Picon (1898-1992). YIVO Institute, New York, papers of Jacob Mestel, 280 (475-84). Program for a performance by Maurice Schwartz at the Monument national, 1955. Canadian Jewish Congress National Archives, Montreal. **P. 73**: *Olivier Guimond Sr., star of the Monument national. Roméo Gariepy Fonds, Cinémathèque québécoise collection, No. 2001.0784.PH.* **P. 74**: Madame Bolduc (1894-1941). Musée régional de Gaspé, collection Fernande M.-A. Bolduc-Travers. **P. 75**: Marie Gérin-Lajoie (1867-1945). "Fédération nationale Saint-Jean-Baptiste" Fonds, Archives nationales du Québec, P 120, 515, P6. **P. 77**: Striptease artist Lili St. Cyr, circa 1946. Weekend Magazine. National Archives of Canada, PA 115228. **P. 78**: Gratien Gélinas as Fridolin plucking petals from a flower, ca 1945. Gratien Gélinas Fonds, National Archives of Canada, PA 210883. Front cover of the program Gratien Gélinas présente Fridolinons 41, 1941.National Archives of Canada, C-148887. **P. 80**: The Canadian Ambassadors, Club Montmartre, the artists and staff of the Club Montmartre on October 6, 1937. Photo: Roger Janelle. Myron Sutton Fonds, P019/P08. Concordia University Archives Department. A flyer from Connie's Inn, one of the city's foremost jazz clubs circa 1932. Myron Sutton Fonds, scrapbook, volume 1, Concordia University Archives Department, P019. Dancers at the Café Saint-Michel, circa 1949. Tina Brereton, Bernice Jordan and Marie-Claire Germaine were part of the first all-Canadian black chorus line. American Photo, Tina Brereton Collection, P074/P03. Concordia University Archives Department. **P. 81**: Illegal lottery on the Main, circa 1935. "Conrad Poirier" Fonds, Archives nationales du Québec, P48, S1, P5207. **P. 82**: The Main and Ontario in 1952. Archives of the Société de transport de Montréal. **P. 84**: 3536 Saint-Laurent Boulevard. Photograph:

Robert Hébert and Sodart. **P. 86**: Corner St. Lawrence and St. Catherine, circa 1960. Ville de Montréal. Gestion des documents et archives, A31-7. **P. 88**: Poster for the film *Il était une fois dans l'Est*, 1973. André Brassard, director. Cinémathèque québécoise, No. 1988. 0580.AF. **P. 89**: Cover of Mordecai Richler's, *The Apprenticeship of Duddy Kravitz*, Toronto, McClelland & Stewart Ltd., @ 1959, 1989. **P. 90**: Jacket of *The Best of Leonard Cohen*, Sony Music Entertainment, 1997. **P. 91**: Claire Savoie, 1986. Photo by Danielle Bérard. Sculptor Pierre Granche at 4060 Saint-Laurent Boulevard, 1986. Photo by Danielle Bérard. Painter Jacques de Tonnancourt at 4060 Saint-Laurent Boulevard, 1986. Photo by Danielle Bérard. Jean Faucher in his studio at 4060 Saint-Laurent Boulevard, 1986. Photo by Danielle Bérard. **P. 92**: The Cinéma Parallèle in 1992. Photo by Jacques Dufresne. Cinémathèque québécoise collection, No. 1999.0205. PH. Café théâtre la Licorne and the Théâtre de la Manufacture, corner of Saint-Norbert, circa 1981. Photo Mirko Buzolitch, Théâtre de la Manufacture / La Licorne collection. **P. 94**: Collection Stella. Andréanne Charlebois, photograph. **P. 95**: Margie Gillis in full flight. Photograph: Annie Leibovitz. **P. 96**: Festival international Nuits d'Afrique de Montréal. Photograph: Nicole Léger. **P. 101**: The Berson workshop, 1986. Photo by Edward Hillel.

Mixed Sources

Product group from well-managed forests, controlled sources and recycled wood or fiber

www.fsc.org Cert no. SGS-COC-003153
© 1996 Forest Stewardship Council

FSC

MARQUIS

Marquis Book Printing Inc.

Québec, Canada

2009